Contents

1	Introduction	1
2	Chapter 1 Soil and Climate	4
3	Chapter 2 Plan Your Garden	8
4	Chapter 3 Seeds	16
5	Chapter 4 Plants	25
6	Chapter 5 Planting	40
7	Chapter 6 Water	75
8	Chapter 7 Compost and Mulch	91
9	Chapter 8 Fertilizers	109
10	Chapter 9 Garden Care and Maintenance	125
11	Chapter 10 Pests and Insects	137
12	Chapter 11 Weeds	164
13	Chapter 12 Tools	173
14	Chapter 13 Miscellaneous	194
15	Conclusion	202
	About the Author	205

TRAVIS WILDER

94 Gardening Hacks

Discover the Secret Tips and Hacks That Will Make Your Friends Green With Envy

Copyright © 2023 by Travis Wilder

All rights reserved. No part of this publication may be reproduced, stored or transmitted in any form or by any means, electronic, mechanical, photocopying, recording, scanning, or otherwise without written permission from the publisher. It is illegal to copy this book, post it to a website, or distribute it by any other means without permission.

First edition

This book was professionally typeset on Reedsy.
Find out more at reedsy.com

1

Introduction

In the enchanting realm of gardening, there exists a world of infinite possibilities. From cultivating vibrant blooms that dance in the breeze to nurturing luscious fruits that burst with flavor, the art of gardening unveils nature's grandest spectacle. But amidst this captivating tapestry lies a secret, a treasure trove of wisdom that has been passed down through the generations. Welcome to "94 Gardening Hacks," where we embark on a remarkable journey, unearthing the ingenious secrets, time-honored tricks, and transformative techniques that will elevate your gardening prowess to extraordinary heights.

Imagine a garden where every seed sown sprouts with vigor, where every plant thrives with resilience, and where every harvest dazzles with abundance. It's within your grasp, waiting to be discovered through the pages of this book. Whether you're a seasoned horticulturist or just beginning your green-thumb adventure, these 94 gardening hacks will revolutionize the way you approach your patch of earth. Say goodbye to ordinary gardening and prepare to embrace a world of infinite possibilities.

Our journey begins with the foundation of any flourishing garden—the soil. Uncover the secrets of soil enrichment, learning how to transform even the humblest dirt into a nutrient-rich haven that nurtures life. From composting wizardry to the art of natural fertilization, you'll unearth the hidden potential of your garden's very foundation.

As the seasons change, so do the challenges and opportunities presented to gardeners. Fear not, for within these pages, you will discover invaluable insights into the art of seasonal gardening. Learn how to harness the magic of each season, turning your garden into an ever-evolving masterpiece. From planting strategies that maximize productivity to weather-proofing techniques that safeguard against nature's whims, you'll possess the knowledge to navigate the shifting tides of gardening with confidence.

But gardening is not merely a science—it's an art form that invites you to express your creativity. Discover the wondrous world of garden design, where landscapes become living canvases. Unleash your imagination as we delve into the principles of color, texture, and symmetry, creating breathtaking compositions that captivate the eye and stir the soul. From small urban oases to sprawling country estates, every gardener can become a masterful artist.

Nature, however, is not without its challenges. Pests and diseases may threaten the very existence of your cherished plants. Fear not, for within these pages, you will unlock the secrets to repelling invaders and keeping your garden healthy and thriving. Discover the art of companion planting, harness the power of natural remedies, and gain insight into the delicate balance between predator and prey. Armed with this knowledge,

INTRODUCTION

you'll preserve the vitality of your garden sanctuary.

As our journey nears its end, we explore the many ways in which gardening extends beyond the boundaries of our own plots. Unleash your green thumb in community gardens, teaching and learning alongside fellow enthusiasts. Embark on sustainable gardening practices, treading lightly upon the earth while embracing the bounties it provides. And when the time comes to harvest, savor the fruits of your labor with delightful recipes that celebrate the flavors of your garden.

"94 Gardening Hacks" is more than a guide; it's an invitation to embark on a transformative journey—a journey that transcends mere gardening and becomes a way of life. So, join me as we dig deep, planting the seeds of wisdom, and watch in awe as your garden blossoms into a symphony of color and life. Let this book be your constant companion, your trusted advisor, and your source of inspiration on the marvelous journey of cultivating nature's wonders.

2

Chapter 1 Soil and Climate

I t all starts from the ground up, so let's start with your garden spot. And that brings us to ...

Garden Hack #1. Know your region: Understanding your local climate and soil type is crucial. What thrives in one area may not in another.

According to the National Centers for Environmental Sciences, the United States is divided into nice climatically distinct regions:

Northwest
Northern Rockies and Plains
Upper Midwest
Ohio Valley
Northeast
Southeast
South
Southwest
West

CHAPTER 1 SOIL AND CLIMATE

Having a good understanding of plants and trees that will (or will not) grow in your corner of the world can mean the difference between gardening success or failure. Pineapples will not grow in Wisconsin outdoors.

And then about that soil type business I mentioned in tip #1 above. More than probably any other factor, soil type and condition will make or break your garden. You can't provide the best growing medium for your plants and garden if you don't know what type of soil you're working with. Throughout the rest of the chapters in this book, we will look at various ways to maximize plant growth utilizing soil amendments.

For now, let's do a simple mason jar soil test to understand the general makeup of your garden soil. Soil consists of three main components - clay, sand, and silt. Loam is a balanced mixture of all three components - 20% clay, 40% silt, 40% sand.

Here's how:

- Obtain a one quart mason jar.
- Fill it ½ way with garden soil - from various locations in the garden or a single location - your choice.
- Fill the jar the rest of the way with water, leaving a little head space for mixing.
- Place a cover on the jar.
- Shake the jar to completely mix the soil and water.
- Allow to stand overnight to settle.
- The three layers of clay, silt, and sand will be clearly visible after the soil is settled. Sand is the heaviest component. It will be the bottom layer. Silt will be the middle layer and

clay particles, being very fine, will be the top layer.
- If your soil is deficient in clay, silt, or sand, try to add more of the deficient component to provide the best growing medium. Adding more organic material to your soil will prove beneficial.

#2: Understand plant hardiness: Each plant has a climate zone where it grows best. Make sure your plants match your local hardiness zone, assuming you are planning an outdoor garden. If you live in colder climates and will be planting indoors or in a greenhouse, you can bend the rules here a bit. Here in Wisconsin, where I live, I've seen lemon trees and humongous tropical plants and bananas being grown in greenhouses.

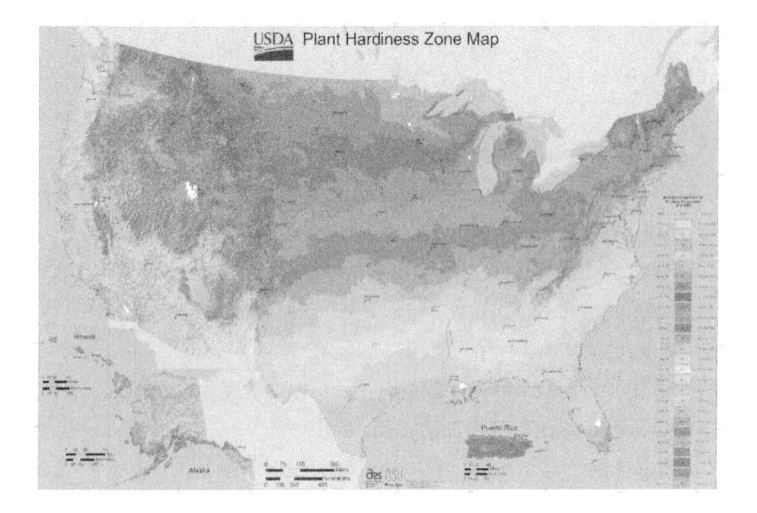

#3: Test your soil: Know your soil's pH and nutrient content. This will guide you on which plants to grow and what type of fertilizer to use. There are several commercially available soil test kits on the market under $30 that will give you a good baseline idea of how your soil measures up for pH and nutrients.

To help your understanding, a neutral pH value (neither acidic nor basic) is 7. As pH increases, your soil is more alkaline (or basic). Alkaline readings go up to 14. As pH decreases, your soil is more acidic. Readings can go down to 0.

Readily available soil test kits, like those referenced above, can also test your soil for nutrients critical for healthy plant growth - potassium, nitrogen, iron, zinc, etc.

#4: Adjust pH levels: Some plants prefer more acidic or alkaline soil. Add lime to increase pH, or add sulfur to decrease it.

3

Chapter 2 Plan Your Garden

#5: Plan your garden: Think about the size, type, and location before you start. Consider the amount of sun exposure, proximity to water sources, and protection from pests.

Thinking very carefully about the size. As summer progresses, so do the weeds. Gardens that are too big to adequately maintain can quickly overwhelm the gardener and cause frustration to the point of giving up. This is a challenge that can really benefit from all hands on deck. If you're a sole gardener, it is even more important to plan a garden size based on your ability to properly maintain it.

The type of garden is very closely related to your choice of garden location. Generally speaking, most gardens will do best with full sun. But, there are always exceptions to every rule. If you're growing a lot of flowers, or plants that are less sun tolerant, be sure to read the plant growing information printed on the plant stake or seed package.

For location, work with what you have available. Don't stress over it. Try to get the best southern exposure that you can for your garden, even if it's just a one-foot wide strip of soil on the edge of a city lot, or a balcony on a high rise in the city.

And always be cognizant of the need for a steady water source. You don't want to have to carry water in buckets to make sure your garden gets water. That gets old fast. Just ask me.

Pests you have with you always. And by the way, not all insects are pests. We'll cover more on that later. There are many ways to deal with pests without toxic industrial strength chemicals and we'll cover many of those in this book.

#6: Use vertical space: If space is limited, consider growing plants on trellises or in hanging baskets.

This is awesome. Many tall, lanky plants, like peas, pole beans, cucumbers and other vines can be grown on vertical trellises or hanging baskets. Talk about space savers! In my garden, I've even had squash and pumpkin vines grow right up, over, and/or through tomato plant supports. And they do just great.

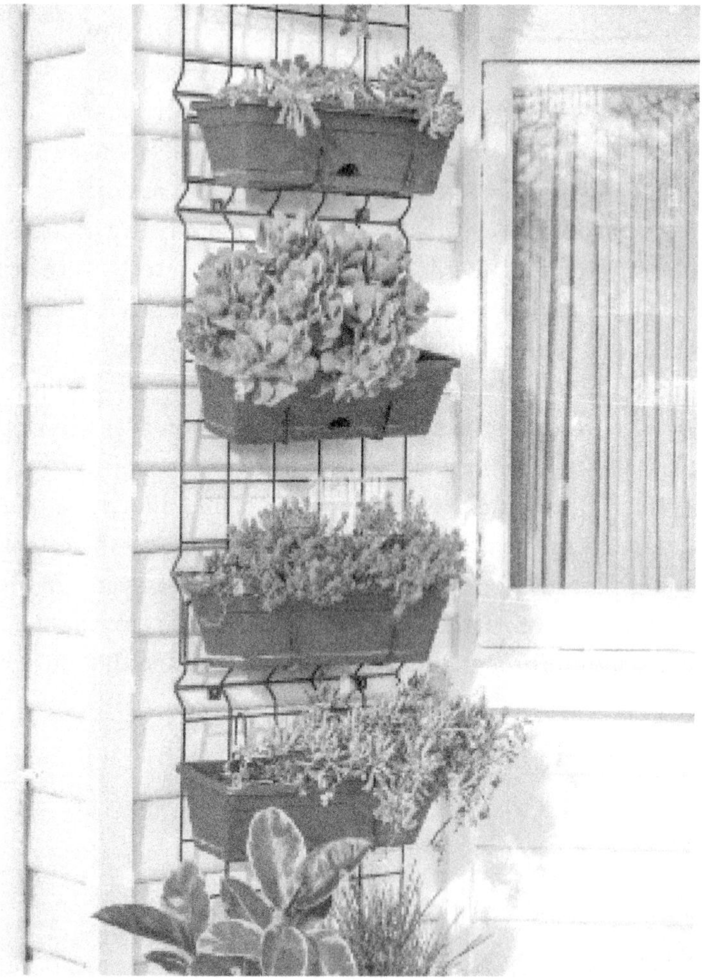

CHAPTER 2 PLAN YOUR GARDEN

#7: Utilize your space: Utilize your space wisely, considering the sunlight and shade in your garden.

Whatever shape your garden takes, remember the sun factor. Sun- loving plants in full sun. You can even plant shorter plants that require less sun in the shade of taller plants or even trees.

#8: Grow what you eat: For vegetable gardens, grow what you love to eat. This will make the gardening process more rewarding.

#9: Try square foot gardening: This method allows you to grow more in less space.

CHAPTER 2 PLAN YOUR GARDEN

#10: Try lasagna gardening: This no-dig, no-till method involves layering organic materials on the surface to create rich soil.

Try these layers to get your lasagna garden producing fast.

- The bottom layer consists of cardboard and/or newspaper for weed control. Wet this layer well.
- Add compost to the second layer.
- Add roughly an inch of straw over the compost.
- Then add both brown (to add carbon) material, like leaves, shredded newspaper, wood shavings/chips. Mix green material (to add nitrogen) like fruit and vegetable scraps and grass clippings. Be sure to mix twice as much brown material as green material.
- Finally, add well composted manure as the top layer. Chicken manure is the highest in nitrogen content.

CHAPTER 2 PLAN YOUR GARDEN

4

Chapter 3 Seeds

#11: Start seeds indoors: This gives your plants a head start and extends your growing season.

In colder climates, seeds can be started indoors in January or February. As weather begins to moderate, plants can then be moved to an outdoor cold frame with southern exposure for a nice greenhouse effect.

In warmer climates, seeds can be started right outside.
Try this Eggshell Seed Starters Hack:
Materials Needed:

1. Empty eggshells
2. Egg carton
3. Seed starter soil or potting mix
4. Seeds of your choice
5. Spray bottle for watering

Steps:

1. Collect Eggshells: Instead of tossing your eggshells after cooking, save them! You'll want them to be as whole as possible, so try to only break off the top third when initially cracking the egg.
2. Clean the Eggshells: Rinse the empty eggshells with warm water. You can place them back into the egg carton to allow them to dry completely.
3. Prepare the Eggshells: With a needle or a thumbtack, poke a small drainage hole in the bottom of each eggshell.
4. Fill with Soil: Fill each eggshell with seed starter soil or potting mix up to about one quarter inch from the top.
5. Plant Seeds: Follow the seeding instructions specific to the plants you've chosen. Typically, this involves planting 1-2 seeds in each eggshell.
6. Water: Using a spray bottle, mist the soil until it is thoroughly damp but not soaking.
7. Grow: Place the egg carton on a sunny windowsill. Make sure the soil stays moist, but be careful not to overwater.

8. Transplant: Once the seedlings have grown one to two sets of true leaves and after all danger of frost has passed, they can be transplanted outside, eggshell and all. The eggshell will decompose and provide valuable nutrients to the soil.

Using eggshells to start seeds indoors is a fun, environmentally friendly way to give your plants a head start. It's also an excellent project to do with children to teach them about the life cycle of plants.

#12: Save seeds: This is a cost-effective way to keep your favorite plants in the garden year after year.
Seed Drying Hack:
Materials Needed:

1. Ripe fruits or vegetables of the plant you want to save seeds from
2. A sharp knife
3. A spoon
4. Paper towels
5. Small envelopes or glass jars for storage
6. A marker for labeling

Steps:

1. Harvest the Seeds: Choose a ripe fruit or vegetable from your healthiest plants. Slice it open and scoop out the seeds. If it's a tomato or cucumber, for instance, you'll find the seeds inside the watery pulp.
2. Clean the Seeds: Rinse the seeds under warm water to

remove any attached pulp. This step is essential as any leftover fruit matter can cause the seeds to rot.
3. Dry the Seeds: Spread the cleaned seeds out on a paper towel. Make sure they are spread out evenly and not clumped together to allow air to circulate around each seed. Place the paper towel in a cool, dry, and well-ventilated location out of direct sunlight.
4. Wait: Allow the seeds to dry completely. This can take anywhere from a few days to a couple of weeks, depending on the type of seed. You'll know the seeds are dry enough when they can't be dented with a fingernail.
5. Store the Seeds: Once dried, store your seeds in small envelopes or glass jars. Label each with the type of seed and the date they were saved. Store these in a cool, dark place until you're ready to plant.

This simple hack makes seed saving an easy task. It's cost-effective and can help maintain the genetic diversity of your garden. Just remember, seeds from hybrid plants may not produce true to the parent plant, so it's better to save seeds from heirloom or open-pollinated varieties.

#13: Use quality seeds: Invest in good quality seeds to ensure healthy plants.

The Seed Research and Invest Hack:

When it comes to gardening, the foundation of your success lies within the quality of seeds you plant. Good seeds will result in healthy plants, whereas poor-quality or old seeds can lead to weak plants or even fail to germinate at all. Here are some steps to ensure you are investing in quality seeds:

1. Buy from Reputable Sources: Purchase your seeds from well-known and trusted seed companies. These companies are more likely to provide high-quality seeds, and they are often willing to replace seeds that don't germinate.
2. Check Reviews: If purchasing seeds online, always check the reviews and ratings. Past buyers' experiences can give you valuable insights into the quality of seeds you are buying.
3. Avoid Bargain Seeds: While saving money is always nice, seeds are not the place to skimp. Those bargain bin seeds can be old, poorly stored, or not true to type.
4. Look for Heirloom or Open-Pollinated Varieties: These types of seeds will breed true-to-type, meaning the plants will have the same characteristics as the parent plant.
5. Check for Seed Viability: Quality seed companies will list the germination rate and the packed for date. Look for high germination rates and seeds packed for the current or upcoming growing season.
6. Consider the Seed Type: Some seeds are coated with a fungicide or pesticide (often these will be brightly colored like pink, green, or blue). If you aim to garden organically, look for untreated seeds.

Investing in quality seeds might mean spending a bit more upfront, but it pays off in the long run with vigorous plants, less disappointment, and abundant harvests. Remember, your garden is only as good as the seeds you plant!

#14: Use egg cartons for seed starters: They are biodegradable and can be planted directly into the ground.

CHAPTER 3 SEEDS

The Egg Carton Seed Starters Hack:
Materials Needed:

1. An empty cardboard egg carton
2. A pair of scissors
3. Seed starter soil or potting mix
4. Seeds of your choice
5. Spray bottle for watering

Steps:

1. Prepare the Egg Carton: If your egg carton has a lid, you'll want to cut this off. You can reserve it to catch any water drips later.
2. Poke Drainage Holes: Using the tip of your scissors, poke a few small holes in the bottom of each egg cup for drainage.
3. Add Soil: Fill each cup with seed starter soil or potting mix until it's level with the top of the cup.
4. Plant the Seeds: Follow the seed packet instructions to determine how deep to plant each seed. As a general rule of thumb, seeds should be planted about as deep as their size. Cover the seeds with a little more soil once they're in their hole.
5. Water: Using a spray bottle, lightly mist the soil until it's thoroughly damp but not soaking.
6. Position the Carton: Place the egg carton on a sunny windowsill or under grow lights if you have them. Make sure the soil stays moist but not waterlogged, misting lightly as needed.
7. Transplant: Once your seedlings have outgrown their egg cup and have formed their second set of true leaves, they

can be carefully transplanted into a larger pot or directly into your garden. If you're transplanting directly into your garden, you can cut apart the egg carton and plant the entire cup, as the cardboard will decompose naturally in the soil.

This hack is an excellent way to recycle household waste and start your seedlings with little to no extra cost!

#15: Plant in pots with removable sides: This makes it easier to remove plants without damaging their root systems.
The Recycled Milk Carton Seed Starters Hack:
Materials Needed:

1. Empty milk or juice cartons
2. A pair of scissors or a utility knife
3. Seed starting mix
4. Seeds of your choice
5. Duct tape
6. Spray bottle for watering

Steps:

1. Prepare the Carton: Cut the carton in half lengthwise. You'll end up with two long, shallow containers.
2. Poke Drainage Holes: Use your scissors or utility knife to poke several drainage holes in the bottom of each half of the carton.
3. Add Soil: Fill the carton halves with seed starting mix to about an inch from the top.
4. Plant the Seeds: Follow the planting instructions for

your specific seeds to determine how deep to plant them. Usually, the seeds should be planted as deep as their size. Cover the seeds with a little extra soil.
5. Water: Using a spray bottle, mist the soil until it is moist but not soaking.
6. Grow: Place the cartons in a sunny spot or under grow lights, if you have them. Keep the soil evenly moist by misting as needed.
7. Transplant: Once the seedlings have grown one to two sets of true leaves, they're ready to be transplanted. At this point, you can carefully cut the side of the carton to remove the seedlings, minimizing root disturbance. If you're transplanting into a larger pot, simply place the seedling in the new pot and fill around it with potting mix. If you're transplanting outdoors, place the seedling in a hole that's deep and wide enough to accommodate the root system, backfill with soil, and water well.

This hack is a great way to reuse milk cartons and give your seedlings a stress-free start to their life! Plus, it's a fun project to do with children to teach them about the life cycle of plants.

#16: Use a sponge in pots: Place a sponge at the bottom of a plant pot to help retain moisture.
The Sponge Moisture Retention Hack:
Materials Needed:

1. A clean, unused sponge
2. A pot with a drainage hole
3. Potting mix
4. Your chosen plant or seeds

Steps:

1. Prepare the Sponge: Take your clean sponge and soak it in water until it's thoroughly saturated.
2. Place the Sponge: Put the wet sponge in the bottom of your pot, flat side down. If you have a larger pot, you may need more than one sponge.
3. Add Potting Mix: Fill the rest of the pot with your potting mix.
4. Plant: Plant your seeds or transplant your plant into the pot, following usual planting instructions.
5. Water: After planting, water as you usually would. The sponge will absorb and hold onto the excess water, then release it back into the soil as it dries out.

This hack is particularly useful for plants that enjoy consistently moist (but not waterlogged) soil, or for when you're going away for a few days and want to make sure your plants don't dry out. It's a great way to reduce the frequency of watering and ensure your plants get a consistent supply of water. Plus, it's a fantastic way to repurpose an old sponge!

Just make sure the sponge you use is free from any detergents or chemicals, which could harm your plants. An all-natural, biodegradable sponge would be ideal. Also, this hack is not a substitute for regular watering or proper plant care. Keep an eye on your plant's health and adjust your care routine as needed.

5

Chapter 4 Plants

#17 Choose the right plants: Some plants require more care than others. If you're a beginner, opt for low-maintenance plants.

The Right Plant, Right Place Hack:

When it comes to gardening, one size definitely doesn't fit all.

Different plants have different needs when it comes to light, water, soil, and care. Here are some steps to help you choose the right plants for your garden:

1. Assess Your Environment: Look at your garden and note the conditions. How much sunlight does it get? Is the soil sandy or clay-like? Is it well-drained or does water pool? Also, consider your climate and the hardiness zone you live in.
2. Consider Your Lifestyle: How much time do you have to devote to your garden? If you're a busy person, you'll want to choose low-maintenance plants. If you enjoy the ritual of daily watering, pruning, and fertilizing, you might opt for plants that require more care.
3. Do Your Research: Once you have an idea of your garden's conditions and your available time, do some research. Look for plants that thrive under the conditions you can provide. There are plenty of resources online, or you could ask at a local nursery or gardening club.
4. Start Small: Especially if you're a beginner gardener, start small. Choose a few plants that you're confident you can care for, and expand your garden as your confidence grows.
5. Trial and Error: Finally, understand that gardening is a process of trial and error. Some plants will thrive while others might not, and that's okay. Learn from the experience and adjust your plant choices as needed.

Remember, a plant that's well-suited to its environment will be healthier and require less care in the long run. This is not only good for the plant, but it's also good for you, saving you time and effort. So take the time to choose the right plant for the right place – your garden will thank you for it!

#18 Companion planting: Some plants grow better next to specific others. For example, marigolds deter pests from tomatoes.

The Companion Planting Hack:

Companion planting is the strategic placement of different plant species near one another to take advantage of their natural properties, whether it's deterring pests, enhancing growth, or attracting beneficial insects. Here's how you can implement it:

1. Do Your Research: Start by researching which plants make good companions. For instance, tomatoes do well with basil and marigolds, but don't get along with potatoes. Carrots and leeks are good together as the smell of leeks deters the carrot fly, and the smell of carrots deters the leek moth.
2. Plan Your Garden: Draw a plan of your garden and decide where to plant each species. Consider factors like sunlight and water requirements, in addition to companion relationships. Some plants can be intercropped (planted in between rows of another crop), while others might need to be a certain distance apart.
3. Plant Your Garden: When planting time comes, follow your plan. Remember to rotate crops each season if possible, as this helps prevent the buildup of diseases and pests.
4. Observe and Adjust: Monitor your garden regularly to see how your plants are doing. If a certain combination

doesn't seem to be working, don't be afraid to try something different next season.

Remember, companion planting is an art as well as a science, and it can take some trial and error to find what works best for your specific garden conditions. However, when done correctly, it can lead to a healthier and more productive garden, and it's a great way to make the most of your space!

#19 Rotate crops: If you're growing vegetables, rotating crops helps prevent depletion of soil nutrients.
The Crop Rotation Hack:
Crop rotation is a practice in gardening and farming where different plant families are planted in different areas of the garden each season. This is a fantastic way to manage soil fertility and to help avoid or reduce problems with soil-borne diseases and certain pests.
Here's how you can implement it:

1. Know Your Plant Families: Understand the different plant families. For instance, tomatoes, peppers, eggplants, and potatoes are all part of the nightshade family and should be rotated together. Similarly, beans and peas are in the legume family and can be planted where nitrogen-loving plants, like the cabbage family (cabbage, kale, broccoli, Brussels sprouts), were the previous season.
2. Plan Your Garden: At the start of each season (or year), plan your garden with rotation in mind. If you had tomatoes in one bed this year, plan to plant them in a different bed next year.
3. Maintain a Garden Journal: Keeping track of what you

planted where each year can be a huge help in planning crop rotation. Make a simple sketch of your garden and note what you planted where. Refer back to this when planning your garden for the next season.
4. Practice a 3- or 4-Year Rotation: Try not to plant the same family of crops in the same place for at least three to four years. This helps interrupt pest and disease life cycles and gives the soil a chance to recover and rebuild nutrients.
5. Supplement with Compost and Organic Matter: Even with crop rotation, it's still essential to feed your soil. Add compost and other organic matter each season to ensure your plants have the nutrients they need.

Remember, crop rotation is an effective and organic method to reduce pests and diseases while boosting your garden's overall health. It's a bit of a long-term strategy, but the health of your soil and plants will definitely benefit from this practice!

#20 Consider native plants: These are adapted to your local climate and soil, requiring less maintenance than exotic species.

The Native Plants Hack:

Native plants are those that naturally occur in your region and have adapted to the local climate, soil, and wildlife over thousands of years. These plants often make a better choice for the garden than exotic species. Here's why:

1. They're Easier to Grow: Native plants have evolved to thrive in your area, meaning they're adapted to the local climate and soil conditions. They're likely to be more tolerant of your region's weather, whether that's a dry summer, a wet winter, or a cold snap.

2. They Support Local Wildlife: Native plants provide habitat and food for local wildlife like bees, butterflies, birds, and beneficial insects. They often offer a richer source of nectar or food than exotic plants.
3. They're Low-Maintenance: Because they're adapted to your area's conditions, native plants usually require less care than exotics. They often need less water, less fertilizer, and are more resistant to local pests and diseases.
4. They Preserve the Local Ecosystem: Planting native helps to preserve the biodiversity of your local area. This is especially important as natural habitats are increasingly threatened by urban development.

Here's how you can incorporate native plants in your garden:

- Know Your Region: Research which plants are native to your area. Your local extension service or a nearby nursery specializing in native plants can be good resources.
- Choose the Right Plants for Your Site: Just because a plant is native doesn't mean it will thrive in all conditions. Some prefer sun, some shade, some dry conditions, and others wet. Select plants that are suitable for your specific garden's conditions.
- Start Small: If you're new to native plant gardening, start small. Choose a few plants to begin with and gradually add more as you become confident.

Remember, gardening with native plants can be a rewarding experience, providing you with a beautiful, low-maintenance garden that also supports your local ecosystems!

#21 Try heirloom varieties: They often have better flavor and pest resistance.

The Heirloom Varieties Hack:

Heirloom plants are varieties that have been passed down through generations because of their valued characteristics. Unlike hybrid varieties, they are open-pollinated, which means you can save their seeds and they will grow true to type. Here's why and how to use them in your garden:

1. Flavor and Diversity: Heirloom varieties often have superior flavor and texture compared to many commercial varieties. They also come in a wider range of sizes, colors, and shapes, which can make your garden and your plate more interesting!
2. Adaptation: Over time, heirloom varieties have adapted to local growing conditions, making them a resilient choice for your garden.
3. Preserving Genetic Diversity: By growing heirlooms, you contribute to the preservation of plant genetic diversity, which is vital for food security and the health of the environment.
4. Seed Saving: Heirlooms allow you to save and share seeds year after year, keeping traditions alive and reducing your seed costs.

Here's how to get started with heirloom varieties:

Choose Your Heirlooms: Look for seed suppliers who specialize in heirlooms. Pick varieties that are suitable for your growing conditions and that offer the characteristics (flavor, size, color, etc.) you're looking for.

Plant and Care for Them: Plant and care for your heirlooms

as you would any other plant, following the supplier's instructions.

Save Your Seeds: At the end of the season, select healthy plants and save their seeds for next year. Make sure to dry and store seeds properly to ensure their viability.

Share and Swap: Share or swap your seeds with other gardeners to try new varieties and keep these heirlooms circulating in the gardening community.

Remember, growing heirloom varieties can be a rewarding way to connect with gardening traditions, add diversity to your garden, and play a part in conserving our planet's genetic diversity!

#22 Inspect plants before buying: Check for signs of disease or pests.

The Plant Inspection Hack:

When buying plants, taking the time to inspect them thoroughly can save you a lot of headaches down the road. Healthy plants will grow better, and they won't bring diseases or pests into your garden. Here's how to do a proper inspection:

1. Check the Foliage: Look at the leaves of the plant. They should be vibrant and free of spots, discoloration, or signs of insect damage such as holes or chew marks. Also, check the underside of the leaves, a common hiding place for pests.
2. Inspect the Stem and Trunk: The stem or trunk should be sturdy and well-formed. Watch for signs of disease or pests, like sores, cankers, or unusual bumps.
3. Examine the Root System: If possible, take a look at the roots. They should be white or light-colored and spread

evenly throughout the soil. Dark, mushy, or sparse roots can be signs of root disease or poor care.
4. Look for Pests: Be on the lookout for signs of pests. This might include the pests themselves, or their eggs, webs, droppings, or the damage they cause.
5. Assess the Overall Vigor: Healthy plants generally look vigorous and strong. Avoid plants that look wilted, yellowed, or sparse.
6. Smell the Plant: A foul odor can sometimes indicate a fungal or bacterial disease. Healthy plants usually have a fresh, earthy smell.

By carefully inspecting plants before you buy, you can ensure you're bringing home plants that have the best chance of thriving, and you'll avoid introducing new pests or diseases into your existing garden. Don't be afraid to pass up a plant that doesn't meet your standards - it's worth waiting for a healthier specimen!

#23 Experiment: Try different plants and methods to see what works best in your garden.

The Garden Experiment Hack:

One of the great joys of gardening is discovering what works best in your unique space. Experimentation can lead to a more productive, beautiful, and satisfying garden. Here's how to make your garden a successful lab:

1. Try New Plants: Each season, consider planting a few new varieties of flowers, vegetables, or herbs. You might find new favorites, and it's a great way to increase biodiversity in your garden.

2. Test Different Methods: Try out different gardening methods, like raised beds, container gardening, vertical gardening, or permaculture. Each has its own advantages and might offer solutions to issues you've been facing.
3. Rotate Crops: Try rotating your crops, even in a small vegetable garden. This can help improve soil health and reduce pest and disease issues.
4. Experiment with Companions: Try different combinations of companion plants to see which pairings work best in your garden.
5. Adjust Watering and Fertilizing: Experiment with different watering or fertilizing schedules to see what your plants respond to best.
6. Keep a Garden Journal: Record your experiments, observations, and plant performances. This invaluable tool will help you learn from both your successes and failures.
7. Be Patient and Observant: Sometimes, the results of your experiments may not be apparent right away. Be patient, observe closely, and adjust as necessary.

Remember, every garden is unique, and what works for one gardener might not work for another. The most successful gardens are often the result of years of trial, error, and learning. So don't be afraid to try new things and take risks. Happy experimenting!

#24 Use disease-resistant varieties: This will reduce the need for pesticides.

The Disease-Resistant Varieties Hack:

Disease-resistant plants are those that are less likely to get certain common diseases. These varieties can be a great asset in your garden, making your gardening experience easier and more successful. Here's why and how to use them:

1. Less Work, More Enjoyment: Disease-resistant varieties typically require less work in terms of disease prevention and treatment. This leaves more time for you to enjoy your garden.
2. Reduced Need for Chemicals: Using disease-resistant varieties can reduce the need for chemical fungicides, making your garden safer for you, your family, and local wildlife.
3. Improved Harvests: Disease-resistant vegetables often yield more productive harvests because the plants stay healthy throughout the growing season.

Here's how to get started with disease-resistant varieties:

Know Your Garden's Diseases: Pay attention to what diseases tend to occur in your garden. Do you often see powdery mildew, black spot, or blight?

Research Varieties: Look for varieties that are resistant to the diseases you often encounter. Seed catalogs and plant tags often provide this information.

Buy From Reputable Sources: Purchase your seeds or plants from reputable nurseries or seed companies. They should be able to provide information about the disease resistance of their offerings.

Rotate Your Crops: Even with disease-resistant varieties, it's still a good idea to practice crop rotation. This can help prevent the buildup of disease pathogens in the soil.

Remember, 'disease-resistant' doesn't mean 'disease-proof'. You'll still need to provide proper care for your plants, and monitor them for signs of disease. But disease-resistant varieties can give you a significant leg up in keeping your garden healthy and thriving!

#25 Mix in annuals with perennials: This will give your garden color throughout the season.

The Mixed Planting Hack:

Integrating both annuals (plants that complete their life cycle in one year) and perennials (plants that live for multiple years) in your garden can offer multiple benefits. It can maximize your garden's visual appeal, extend your blooming season, and enhance biodiversity. Here's how:

1. Extended Bloom Times: Perennials often have specific bloom times, but by adding annuals that bloom at different times, you can ensure something is always putting on a show in your garden.
2. Filling in the Gaps: Annuals are great for filling in gaps between perennials, providing color and interest while the perennials are getting established or are out of bloom.
3. Variety of Colors and Textures: By mixing annuals and perennials, you can play with different color combinations and textures each year, adding excitement and change to your garden design.
4. Supporting Pollinators: A mix of annuals and perennials can provide a longer and more diverse supply of nectar and pollen for bees, butterflies, and other pollinators.

Here's how to get started with mixed plantings:

Plan Your Planting: Start by identifying the perennials you want to keep as the backbone of your garden. Then, think about where you could add annuals for extra color and interest.

Choose Your Plants: Select a mix of annuals and perennials that are suitable for your garden's conditions (sunlight, soil type, climate, etc.). Try to choose a variety of plants that bloom at different times to extend the flowering season.

Plant Carefully: Plant your perennials with enough space to grow and spread. You can fill in the gaps with annuals, but make sure they won't crowd out your perennials.

Try Different Combinations: Don't be afraid to experiment with different combinations of plants each year. That's part of the fun of using annuals!

Remember, a mix of annuals and perennials can bring a dynamic and vibrant feel to your garden, offering changing scenery from season to season and year to year!

#26 Choose plants suited to your soil: Not all plants can thrive in all soil types.

The Soil-Suitable Planting Hack:

Soil type can have a profound effect on the health and vitality of your garden. Selecting plants that thrive in your particular soil type will not only ensure their success but will also reduce the amount of work you have to do to amend the soil. Here's how:

1. Understand Your Soil: Your soil could be sandy, clay, loamy, or somewhere in between. Each type has its own characteristics - sandy soil drains quickly, clay soil retains water, and loamy soil is an ideal balance of the two. You can identify your soil type by feeling it and observing how quickly water drains through it.
2. Research Suitable Plants: Once you know your soil type,

research which plants naturally thrive in those conditions. For instance, lavender and rosemary do well in sandy soil, while ferns and astilbe prefer clay soil.
3. Look at Local Plants: Take a look at what's growing well in your area, in gardens, parks, or the wild. This can give you a good idea of what might thrive in your garden.
4. Respect the Plant's Preferences: Even if you love a particular plant, if it's not suited to your soil type, it may struggle to grow and be more susceptible to pests and diseases. Instead, try to find similar alternatives that are better suited to your soil.
5. Be Cautious with Soil Amendments: While it's possible to amend soil to suit certain plants, this can be a lot of work and isn't always sustainable in the long term. It's usually easier and more effective to work with your soil rather than against it.

By choosing plants suited to your soil type, you'll be setting your garden up for success. You'll likely find your plants are healthier, require less maintenance, and provide more enjoyment in your gardening journey!

#27 Use hydrogen peroxide to help root cuttings: It prevents rot and encourages root growth.
   The Hydrogen Peroxide Rooting Hack:
   Hydrogen peroxide is not only a common household disinfectant, but it can also aid in rooting plant cuttings. Its chemical makeup (H_2O_2) provides an extra oxygen molecule that can promote root development and help prevent disease. Here's how to use it:

1. Prepare Your Peroxide Solution: Add 1 teaspoon of 3% hydrogen peroxide to 1 cup of water. Stir until well combined.
2. Prep Your Cuttings: Take a cutting from a healthy plant. Make the cut just below a node (where the leaves attach to the stem). Remove all but the top few leaves.
3. Soak Your Cutting: Submerge the cut end of your plant cutting in the hydrogen peroxide solution for a few minutes.
4. Plant Your Cutting: After soaking, immediately transfer the cutting into a pot filled with sterile, damp soil or a soilless rooting medium. You may also choose to dip the cutting in rooting hormone before planting, but this is optional.
5. Water with Peroxide Solution: Use the remaining hydrogen peroxide solution to water the cutting. It will help to keep disease at bay and promote root development.
6. Keep it Humid: Cover the cutting with a clear plastic bag or place it in a mini greenhouse to maintain high humidity. Remember to open the cover every few days to let in fresh air.
7. Wait for Root Development: In a few weeks, roots should begin to form. You can gently tug on the cutting to feel for resistance, which indicates that roots are growing. Once the roots are well established, you can transplant the cutting to a larger pot or garden.

Remember, hydrogen peroxide can be harmful in higher concentrations, so stick to the recommended amounts and keep it out of reach of children and pets. Happy planting!

6

Chapter 5 Planting

#28 Practice succession planting: This helps ensure a continuous harvest throughout the growing season.

The Succession Planting Hack:

Succession planting is a gardening practice that ensures a continuous supply of crops throughout the growing season.

CHAPTER 5 PLANTING

This method maximizes the use of your garden space and extends your harvest. Here's how to get started:

1. Understand the Concept: Succession planting involves planting crops in intervals. Once a crop is harvested, you immediately plant another crop in its place. You can repeat the same crop or choose different ones.
2. Plan Your Crops: Choose crops that mature quickly for best results. Lettuces, radishes, and green beans are good examples. Also, consider crops that can be planted later in the season, like fall-harvested vegetables.
3. Consider Crop Needs: Make sure the succeeding crop has the same sunlight and soil requirements as the preceding one. You wouldn't want to plant a sun-loving crop where a shade-loving crop just came out.
4. Prepare Your Seeds: If you're planting fast-growing crops, start a new batch of seeds indoors every 2-3 weeks. This will ensure you have young plants ready to go into the garden as soon as the previous crops are harvested.
5. Replenish the Soil: Each time you harvest and remove a crop, replenish the nutrients in the soil by adding compost or a balanced organic fertilizer.
6. Keep Records: Keeping a garden journal can help you plan your succession planting better. Note down when you planted each crop, when it was harvested, and any other observations. This will help you refine your timings and crop choices for the next growing season.

Remember, succession planting requires a bit more planning and effort than planting all at once, but the rewards are well worth it. With this method, you'll maximize your garden's productivity and enjoy fresh, home-grown food for a longer period!

#29 Plant in raised beds: These improve drainage and can make gardening easier on your back.

The Raised Bed Planting Hack:

Raised bed gardening is a productive and convenient way to grow a variety of plants. These freestanding beds are filled with soil and plants, providing numerous advantages over traditional in-ground gardening. Here's why:

1. Improved Soil Condition: Raised beds give you control over the soil in which you're planting. You can fill them with the perfect soil mix, making them great for areas with poor or compacted soil.
2. Better Drainage: The elevated soil in a raised bed drains more efficiently. This can be especially beneficial in regions where rainfall is heavy and soil tends to become waterlogged.
3. Ease of Access: Raised beds are easier on the back and knees because they reduce the need to bend over. This can make gardening more accessible for people with physical limitations.
4. Extended Growing Season: The soil in raised beds warms up more quickly in the spring, offering a head start on the growing season. In addition, by covering the beds with plastic, you can further extend the season.
5. Pest and Weed Control: Raised beds can make it harder for pests to reach your plants and can reduce the invasion of some weeds.
6. Crop Rotation Made Easy: If you have multiple raised beds,

CHAPTER 5 PLANTING

it's straightforward to practice crop rotation, which can help prevent the buildup of soil-borne pests and diseases.

Here's how to get started:

Choose the Right Material: Raised beds can be made from a variety of materials including wood, stone, metal, or even recycled plastic. Choose a material that suits your garden's aesthetics and your budget.

Select the Right Size: Ideally, the width of the bed should allow you to comfortably reach the middle from either side, and the length can be whatever fits your garden space.

Plan Your Plants: Consider what you want to grow. Certain plants will require deeper beds than others, so do your research beforehand.

Fill with Quality Soil: Use a mix of topsoil, compost, and other organic matter to fill your raised beds. This will provide a rich environment for your plants to grow.

Remember, raised bed gardening might require an upfront investment of time and resources, but the pay-off in crop yield, ease of maintenance, and gardening enjoyment can be well worth the effort!

#30 Avoid tilling: It can destroy soil structure and beneficial soil organisms.

The No-Till Gardening Hack:

No-till gardening is a method that involves minimal disturbance of the soil. Instead of tilling or overturning the soil, you work with its natural structure and layers. This approach offers several benefits for your garden and the environment. Here's why:

1. Preservation of Soil Structure: Tilling disrupts the natural structure of the soil, which can lead to compaction and erosion. By avoiding tilling, you maintain the soil's natural composition and prevent the breakdown of its beneficial microorganisms.
2. Improved Soil Health: No-till gardening promotes a thriving soil ecosystem. The beneficial organisms, earthworms, and microorganisms present in undisturbed soil contribute to nutrient cycling, soil aeration, and organic matter decomposition.
3. Reduced Weed Growth: Tilling can bring dormant weed seeds to the surface, leading to increased weed growth. No-till gardening disturbs fewer weed seeds, minimizing weed emergence and reducing the need for excessive weeding.
4. Water Conservation: Tilling can disrupt the soil's ability to retain moisture, leading to increased water evaporation and the need for more frequent watering. No-till gardening helps conserve water by preserving the soil's moisture-holding capacity.
5. Erosion Prevention: The structure and layering of undisturbed soil help prevent erosion by providing a stable environment for plant roots and improving water infiltration.

Here's how to implement no-till practices in your garden:

Sheet Mulching: Instead of tilling, use a sheet mulching method to suppress weeds and build soil fertility. Layer organic materials like cardboard, newspaper, straw, or leaves over the soil surface and plant directly into it.

Use Raised Beds: Raised beds allow you to create a controlled environment for your plants without disturbing the soil underneath. Fill them with a quality soil mix and add compost regularly to maintain fertility.

Practice Crop Rotation: Rotate your crops each season to help manage pests and diseases while keeping the soil structure intact.

Mulch: Apply organic mulch, such as straw, wood chips, or leaves, around your plants to suppress weeds, retain moisture, and maintain soil temperature.

By embracing no-till gardening, you can foster a healthy and resilient garden ecosystem while minimizing soil erosion, conserving water, and reducing the need for excessive weeding and watering.

#31 Know when to plant: Each plant has an optimal time for planting. Understanding this ensures a healthier plant.

The Timing for Planting Hack:

Timing is crucial when it comes to planting in your garden. Planting too early or too late can have a significant impact on your plant's growth and productivity. To ensure successful planting, consider the following factors:

1. Know Your Climate: Understand your local climate and the average frost dates for your region. This will provide a baseline for determining when to start planting.
2. Read Seed Packets or Plant Tags: Seed packets and plant tags often include specific information about the ideal planting time for each variety. They may indicate the number of weeks before or after the last frost date to sow seeds or transplant seedlings.
3. Refer to a Gardening Calendar: Consult a gardening calendar or guide specific to your area. These resources provide

recommended planting dates based on the frost dates and the best times for various vegetables, flowers, and herbs.
4. Consider Soil Temperature: Certain plants require specific soil temperatures for optimal germination and growth. Use a soil thermometer to measure the soil temperature, and refer to planting guides that include soil temperature ranges for different plants.
5. Observe Nature's Cues: Pay attention to natural signs in your garden and surroundings. Look for the emergence of specific plants or the behavior of wildlife, as they can indicate when conditions are favorable for planting.
6. Experiment and Keep Records: Keep a garden journal to record your planting dates and the subsequent growth and performance of your plants. This will help you refine your planting timing in subsequent years.
7. Consider Microclimates: Your garden may have microclimates, such as warmer or cooler areas due to sun exposure, wind patterns, or sheltered spots. Take advantage of these microclimates to extend your growing season or protect sensitive plants from extreme conditions.

Remember, planting timing can vary depending on your specific location and microclimate. By considering factors like frost dates, seed packets, local resources, and nature's cues, you'll be able to determine the best time to plant and increase your chances of a successful and bountiful garden!

#32 Plant perennials: They come back year after year, saving you time and money.

The Perennial Planting Hack:

Adding perennials to your garden can provide numerous

CHAPTER 5 PLANTING

benefits, from long-lasting beauty to low-maintenance care. These plants return year after year, offering a wealth of advantages. Here's why you should consider planting perennials:

1. Longevity and Cost Efficiency: Perennials have a longer lifespan compared to annuals, meaning you'll enjoy their beauty and benefits for many years. While they may require an initial investment, they save you money in the long run by not needing to be replaced each season.
2. Low Maintenance: Once established, perennials generally require less maintenance than annuals. They have developed stronger root systems, making them more resilient to weather fluctuations and requiring less frequent watering.
3. Reduced Weed Competition: Perennials form dense root systems and foliage, minimizing weed growth and competition. As they mature, they shade the soil, hindering weed seed germination and reducing the need for excessive weeding.
4. Eco-Friendly Landscaping: Perennials contribute to sustainable gardening practices. Their deep-rooted systems improve soil structure, increase water infiltration, and prevent erosion. They also provide habitat and food sources for pollinators, beneficial insects, and wildlife.
5. Yearly Bloom Cycle: Many perennials have a specific blooming period, offering a burst of color and fragrance during their season. By selecting a variety of perennials with different bloom times, you can ensure your garden is continually in bloom throughout the growing season.
6. Versatility and Adaptability: Perennials come in various sizes, colors, and textures, allowing you to create diverse

and visually appealing garden landscapes. They adapt to different garden styles, from formal beds to wildflower meadows, and thrive in a range of growing conditions.

7. Opportunity for Division and Sharing: As perennials grow and mature, they often form clumps that can be divided and shared with friends and family. This not only enhances your garden but fosters a sense of community and connection with fellow gardeners.

When planning your garden, consider incorporating a mix of perennials to ensure long-lasting beauty, reduced maintenance, and a vibrant, ecologically friendly landscape. With their enduring presence, perennials are a wonderful addition to any garden!

#33 Plant a pollinator garden: This attracts bees, butterflies, and other pollinators, which helps improve your garden's productivity.

The Pollinator Garden Hack:

Pollinator gardens are designed to attract and support essential pollinators like bees, butterflies, and hummingbirds. These gardens not only add beauty to your landscape but also contribute to the health and sustainability of our ecosystem. Here's how to create a thriving pollinator garden:

1. Choose the Right Location: Select a sunny spot in your garden that receives at least 6 hours of direct sunlight each day. Pollinators are generally attracted to areas with ample sunlight.
2. Select Native Plants: Choose a variety of native flowering plants. Native plants have evolved alongside local pollina-

tors, providing them with the nectar, pollen, and habitat they need. Research which plants are native to your region and suit your growing conditions.
3. Plant a Diverse Range of Flowers: Include plants that bloom at different times throughout the growing season. This ensures a continuous source of food for pollinators. Aim for a mix of flowers with different colors, shapes, and sizes to attract a variety of pollinators.
4. Provide Water Sources: Create water sources such as shallow dishes, birdbaths, or a small pond. Place pebbles or stones in the water to provide perching spots for insects. Ensure that the water source is shallow and has a rough surface for them to safely access water.
5. Avoid Pesticides: Minimize or eliminate the use of chemical pesticides, as they can be harmful to pollinators. Opt for natural pest control methods, such as handpicking pests or using organic alternatives.
6. Provide Shelter and Nesting Sites: Incorporate plants that offer shelter and nesting opportunities for pollinators. Plants with dense foliage or grasses provide excellent hiding places and breeding sites for butterflies and other insects.
7. Offer Host Plants: Many butterflies and moths have specific host plants on which they lay their eggs. Research and include host plants for the particular species you want to attract. These plants will serve as a food source for the caterpillars.
8. Create a Continuous Bloom: To ensure a consistent food source, consider planting in clusters or drifts rather than scattering individual plants. This helps pollinators locate and access the flowers more easily.

9. Maintain the Garden: Regularly water, weed, and remove spent flowers to encourage new blooms. Deadheading (removing faded flowers) also stimulates continued blooming.
10. Educate and Inspire: Share the beauty and importance of pollinator gardens with friends, neighbors, and children. Encourage others to create their own pollinator-friendly spaces.

By following these steps, you'll create an inviting oasis for pollinators, contributing to their conservation while enjoying the beauty of your vibrant and buzzing pollinator garden!

#34 Avoid planting in rows: It's inefficient and takes up unnecessary space.

The Non-Row Planting Hack:

Planting in traditional rows is a common practice in gardening, but breaking away from this method can offer several advantages for your garden. Non-row planting, also known as companion planting or intensive planting, maximizes space, enhances biodiversity, and promotes healthier plants. Here's how to do it:

1. Maximize Space: Non-row planting allows you to utilize space more efficiently. By reducing the space between plants and using intercropping techniques, you can grow a larger variety of crops in the same area.
2. Increased Yield: Planting closely together creates a microclimate that retains moisture and shades the soil, reducing weed growth and conserving water. This leads to increased yields and more productive gardens.

3. Weed Suppression: Planting densely shades the soil, which naturally suppresses weed growth by limiting sunlight. The tight spacing also reduces available space for weeds to establish themselves.
4. Natural Pest Control: Intercropping and companion planting can help deter pests naturally. Certain plants repel pests, while others attract beneficial insects that prey on pests. This creates a balanced ecosystem, reducing the need for chemical interventions.
5. Improved Soil Health: Non-row planting improves soil structure and fertility. The dense planting helps to prevent erosion and adds organic matter to the soil through the natural decomposition of plant material.
6. Crop Diversity: Planting in a mixed, non-row style promotes biodiversity by incorporating different crops and varieties. This enhances ecological resilience and reduces the risk of widespread crop failure due to pests or diseases.
7. Aesthetic Appeal: Non-row planting can create visually appealing gardens, with a diverse mix of plants, textures, and colors. It can also provide a natural, "wild" look, which can be attractive and inviting.

Here's how to implement non-row planting in your garden:

Plan Your Garden Layout: Designate planting areas based on the requirements and compatibility of different crops. Consider factors such as sunlight, soil type, and water needs.

Choose Complementary Plants: Select plants that have complementary growth habits, nutrient requirements, or pest-repellent properties. Research companion planting to find suitable combinations.

Utilize Vertical Space: Grow vining plants on trellises or

supports to make the most of your garden's vertical space, further increasing planting options.

Consider Succession Planting: Rather than planting everything at once, stagger your planting to ensure a continuous supply of fresh produce throughout the growing season.

By embracing non-row planting techniques, you'll maximize your garden's productivity, enhance biodiversity, and create a visually appealing and harmonious garden space!

#35 Consider container gardening: If you're short on space, many plants grow well in pots.

The Container Gardening Hack:

Container gardening offers a versatile and convenient way to grow plants, even in limited spaces. Whether you have a small balcony, patio, or windowsill, you can create a thriving garden using containers. Here's how:

1. Choose the Right Containers: Select containers with adequate drainage holes to prevent waterlogging. Ensure they are the appropriate size for the plants you want to grow, considering both their current and future size.
2. Select the Proper Soil: Use a high-quality potting mix that provides good drainage while retaining moisture. Avoid using garden soil, as it tends to be heavy and may not drain well in containers.
3. Consider Planting Depth: Be mindful of the root depth requirements of your plants. Choose containers that offer enough depth for proper root development.
4. Match Plants with Containers: Consider the mature size and growth habits of your plants when selecting containers. Avoid overcrowding by choosing appropriate-sized

pots for each plant.
5. Provide Adequate Watering: Container plants often require more frequent watering than those in the ground. Check the soil moisture regularly and water when the top inch feels dry. Ensure that excess water can drain freely.
6. Apply Mulch: Use mulch on the surface of container soil to help retain moisture and regulate soil temperature. Organic mulches like straw or wood chips work well.
7. Fertilize Regularly: Nutrients in container soil can deplete quickly, so regularly feed your plants with a balanced liquid fertilizer or slow-release granules, following the package instructions.
8. Ensure Proper Drainage: Elevate containers using pot feet or blocks to ensure adequate drainage and prevent water from pooling underneath.
9. Consider Microclimates: Containers can create microclimates due to sun exposure and proximity to walls or structures. Understand the unique conditions of each location and choose plants accordingly.
10. Rotate and Refresh: Rotate your container plants periodically to ensure even growth and sun exposure. Refresh the soil annually by removing the top layer and replacing it with fresh potting mix.
11. Be Mindful of Pests: Monitor your container plants for pests regularly. Inspect both the foliage and soil, and take necessary steps to control any pest infestations.

Container gardening offers flexibility, mobility, and the ability to garden in small spaces. With proper care and attention, you can enjoy a bountiful and beautiful garden right on your doorstep!

#36 Don't forget about indoor gardening: Houseplants can purify the air and bring nature indoors.

The Indoor Gardening Hack:

Indoor gardening is a fantastic way to bring greenery, beauty, and even food production into your home. Whether you have a small apartment or want to grow plants during the colder months, indoor gardening can be a rewarding experience. Here's how to get started:

1. Evaluate Light Conditions: Assess the available light in your indoor space. Most plants require bright, indirect light to thrive. Place your indoor garden near windows or consider using artificial grow lights for plants that require more intense light.
2. Choose the Right Plants: Select plants that are well-suited for indoor growing conditions. Some popular indoor plants include pothos, spider plants, peace lilies, herbs, and small vegetables like cherry tomatoes or lettuce. Research their specific light, temperature, and humidity requirements.
3. Optimize Soil and Containers: Use a well-draining potting mix specifically designed for indoor plants. Ensure your containers have drainage holes to prevent waterlogging. Consider the size of your plants and choose appropriately-sized pots that allow for root development.
4. Water Properly: Indoor plants can be prone to overwatering. Check the moisture level of the soil regularly and water only when the top inch feels dry. Avoid water stagnation in saucers by emptying excess water after watering.
5. Provide Humidity: Indoor environments tend to be drier,

especially during winter months with central heating. Increase humidity by placing a tray of water near your plants or using a humidifier. Grouping plants together can also create a microclimate with higher humidity.

6. Fertilize Mindfully: Indoor plants may benefit from regular fertilization, especially during the growing season. Use a balanced liquid fertilizer and follow the recommended dosage. Be cautious not to over-fertilize, as it can damage the plants.
7. Prune and Maintain: Regularly inspect your indoor plants for any signs of pests, disease, or dead/damaged foliage. Prune as needed to maintain their shape and remove any unhealthy parts. Wipe the leaves with a damp cloth to remove dust and enhance their appearance.
8. Rotate and Rejuvenate: Rotate your plants periodically to ensure even light exposure and prevent them from leaning towards the light source. Refresh your indoor garden by replacing tired or struggling plants with new additions.
9. Enjoy the Benefits: Indoor gardening provides more than just beautiful plants. It can enhance air quality, reduce stress, and bring a sense of tranquility to your indoor space. Take time to appreciate the beauty and benefits your indoor garden provides.

Indoor gardening allows you to cultivate a green oasis within your home, even if you have limited outdoor space. With proper care and attention, you can create a thriving indoor garden that brings nature's beauty indoors!

#37 Learn plant spacing: Overcrowded plants can lead to disease and low yields.

The Plant Spacing Hack:
Proper plant spacing is essential for optimal growth, airflow, and overall plant health in your garden. By providing adequate space between plants, you can minimize competition for resources, reduce the risk of diseases, and maximize the potential yield. Here's how to determine and implement effective plant spacing:

1. Read Plant Labels or Seed Packets: Pay attention to the recommended spacing information provided on plant labels or seed packets. It usually indicates the distance needed between plants to ensure healthy growth.
2. Consider Mature Size: Research and understand the expected mature size of each plant. This will help you determine how much space they require to grow to their full potential without overcrowding neighboring plants.
3. Follow Spacing Guidelines: Adhere to the recommended spacing guidelines, especially for plants that require ample airflow, such as leafy greens, to prevent the onset of diseases caused by high humidity and poor air circulation.
4. Account for Planting Techniques: Adjust spacing based on specific planting techniques. For example, if you're planting in hills or clusters, provide enough space for each plant to spread comfortably.
5. Utilize Companion Planting: Incorporate companion planting strategies to optimize space utilization and promote symbiotic relationships between plants. Some combinations, such as tall plants providing shade for smaller ones, can allow for closer spacing.
6. Practice Succession Planting: Incorporate succession planting to make the most of available space. As one

crop is harvested, replant with a new crop to ensure a continuous supply of fresh produce.
7. Consider Plant Height: Take into account the height of plants when determining spacing. Taller plants may cast shadows and affect the sunlight availability for shorter plants. Arrange your garden layout to maximize light exposure for all plants.
8. Thin Seedlings: If you have sown seeds densely, thin out the seedlings once they have grown a few inches tall. This allows each plant to have sufficient room to develop its root system and prevents overcrowding.
9. Monitor and Adjust: Regularly observe your plants as they grow. If you notice overcrowding or stunted growth, consider thinning or transplanting to provide more space.
10. Adapt Based on Varieties: Different plant varieties may have specific spacing requirements. Research and adjust spacing based on the unique needs of the plants you are growing.

By implementing proper plant spacing techniques, you can optimize the health and productivity of your garden, resulting in healthier plants, increased airflow, reduced disease risk, and higher yields of delicious homegrown produce!

#38 Plant in blocks: Instead of rows, plant in blocks to maximize your space.

The Block Planting Hack:

Planting in blocks, also known as square foot gardening or intensive planting, is a strategic method that maximizes space, enhances productivity, and improves pollination in your garden. By grouping plants together in dense blocks, you can optimize resources and achieve higher yields. Here's how to implement block planting in your garden:

1. Plan Your Garden Layout: Divide your garden space into smaller blocks or grids, each typically measuring one square foot or more, depending on the size of your plants. Use string or raised beds to create distinct planting areas.
2. Group Plants Together: Instead of planting in long rows, place plants in tight groupings within each block. This creates a dense and compact arrangement, reducing wasted space and maximizing plant density.
3. Optimize Spacing: Follow recommended plant spacing guidelines for each plant type, considering their mature size and requirements. Arrange plants closely together, leaving just enough space for them to grow without overcrowding.
4. Maximize Resource Utilization: Planting in blocks allows for efficient utilization of resources like water, nutrients, and sunlight. With plants in close proximity, their leaves shade the soil, reducing evaporation and weed growth. Use organic mulch to further conserve moisture and suppress weeds.
5. Encourage Polyculture: Incorporate a mix of compatible plants within each block. This promotes beneficial interactions such as pest control, nutrient sharing, and improved pollination. Companion planting guides can help you identify suitable combinations.
6. Consider Plant Height: Arrange plants based on their height to avoid shading shorter ones. Place taller plants towards the back or center of the block, gradually transitioning to shorter plants towards the front or edges. This

ensures all plants receive adequate sunlight.
7. Support Climbing Plants: Install trellises or stakes within the blocks to support climbing or vining plants. This helps maximize vertical space and prevents sprawling, keeping the plants tidy and easily accessible.
8. Rotate Crops: After harvesting a block, rotate the next set of crops to a different block. This practice helps prevent disease buildup and maintains soil fertility.
9. Sow Successive Plantings: As you harvest a block, replant it immediately with a new batch of seeds or seedlings. This ensures a continuous supply of fresh produce throughout the growing season.
10. Monitor and Maintain: Regularly monitor your block plantings for pests, diseases, or nutrient deficiencies. Address any issues promptly to keep your plants healthy and thriving.

By adopting the block planting method, you can optimize space, improve crop productivity, and create a visually appealing and efficient garden layout. Embrace this technique to make the most of your gardening space while enjoying abundant harvests!

#39 Protect your seedlings: Use cloches or plant protectors for young plants as they are vulnerable to pests and weather changes.

The Seedling Protection Hack:

Protecting seedlings in their early stages is crucial for their successful establishment and growth. Cloches or plant protectors provide a simple and effective solution to shield young plants from adverse weather conditions, pests, and other potential threats. Here's why it's important and how to use them:

1. Weather Protection: Seedlings are often delicate and vulnerable to harsh weather conditions, such as cold temperatures, frost, or strong winds. Cloches or plant protectors act as mini greenhouses, creating a microclimate that shields seedlings from these elements.
2. Pest Defense: Seedlings can attract pests, including insects and small animals, which may nibble on their tender leaves or cause damage to the root system. Cloches and plant protectors act as a physical barrier, preventing pests from reaching the seedlings.
3. Temperature Regulation: Cloches help regulate temperature around the seedlings, providing a slightly warmer environment that promotes faster growth. They can also safeguard against sudden temperature fluctuations that might harm delicate young plants.
4. Enhanced Growth: By creating a protected environment, cloches and plant protectors encourage faster and healthier growth in seedlings. They provide a controlled space with increased humidity, reduced moisture loss, and improved air circulation.

Here's how to use cloches or plant protectors effectively:

- Choose the Right Type: Select a suitable type of cloche or plant protector based on your needs and the size of your seedlings. Options include individual plastic or glass cloches, floating row covers, or even repurposed materials like plastic bottles or milk jugs with the bottoms removed.

- Prepare the Seedbed: Before placing the cloches or plant protectors, prepare the seedbed by removing weeds and loosening the soil. Ensure the soil is moist but not waterlogged.
- Install the Cloches: Gently place the cloches over the seedlings, ensuring they are securely anchored in the soil. For row covers or larger protectors, drape them over the seedbed and secure the edges with rocks, stakes, or clips.
- Monitor and Ventilate: Regularly check the seedlings under the cloches for any signs of excessive heat or humidity buildup. If needed, open or ventilate the cloches during warm periods to prevent overheating or fungal growth.
- Gradual Removal: Gradually acclimate the seedlings to outdoor conditions by gradually removing the cloches or plant protectors over a period of time. This allows the plants to adjust to the outdoor environment without sudden exposure.
- Reuse and Repurpose: Once the seedlings have established and no longer need protection, store the cloches or plant protectors for future use. Properly clean and sanitize them to prevent the spread of diseases.

By providing seedlings with the protection they need, you increase their chances of survival and healthy growth. Cloches and plant protectors offer a practical and affordable solution to safeguard your precious seedlings as they develop into strong, resilient plants.

#40 Plant for all seasons: Choose a variety of plants to ensure your garden is vibrant all year round.

The Year-Round Planting Hack:

Planting for all seasons allows you to enjoy a continuous harvest and a vibrant garden throughout the year. By strategically selecting plants and planning your garden layout, you can ensure there's something growing and thriving in every season. Here's how to achieve a year-round garden:

1. Know Your Hardiness Zone: Determine your hardiness zone to understand the specific climatic conditions of your region. This knowledge will guide you in selecting plants that are suitable for year-round growth in your area.
2. Plan Your Garden Layout: Divide your garden space into sections or areas dedicated to each season. Consider factors such as sunlight exposure, soil conditions, and available space when designing the layout.
3. Choose a Variety of Plants: Select a diverse range of plants that thrive in different seasons. Include cool-season crops like lettuces, spinach, and peas for spring and fall, warm-season crops like tomatoes, peppers, and cucumbers for summer, and cold-hardy crops like kale, Brussels sprouts, and carrots for winter.
4. Succession Planting: Practice succession planting to maximize your harvest throughout the seasons. As one crop is harvested, replant with a new crop to ensure a continuous supply of fresh produce.
5. Utilize Season Extenders: Extend the growing season by utilizing season extenders such as cold frames, row covers, or hoop houses. These structures protect plants from frost and provide a few extra weeks of growing time in spring and fall.
6. Consider Perennials: Incorporate perennial plants that provide year-round interest and productivity. Examples

CHAPTER 5 PLANTING

include fruit trees, berry bushes, perennial herbs, and flowers that bloom across different seasons.
7. Choose Varieties with Varying Maturity Dates: Opt for plant varieties with different maturity dates. This way, you'll have crops maturing at various times, ensuring a continuous harvest throughout the season.
8. Monitor Planting and Harvesting Times: Keep track of planting and harvesting times for each crop. Refer to gardening calendars or guides specific to your region to ensure you're planting at the right time for each season.
9. Protect from Extreme Weather: Be prepared for extreme weather conditions, such as heatwaves, heavy rains, or strong winds, by taking necessary precautions like providing shade, staking tall plants, or providing windbreaks.
10. Maintain Healthy Soil: Regularly replenish and amend your soil with compost or organic matter to ensure it remains fertile and productive throughout the seasons.

By incorporating these strategies, you can achieve a year-round garden that offers a continuous supply of fresh produce and a visually appealing landscape. Embrace the diversity of plants and the joy of gardening in every season!

#41 Grow cover crops: They improve soil health and prevent erosion during the off season.

The Cover Crop Hack:

Cover crops, also known as green manure, offer a range of benefits for your garden. These crops are grown primarily to protect and improve the soil when the main crops are not in season. By following this gardening hack, you can maximize soil health and fertility in your garden:

1. Soil Protection: Cover crops protect the soil from erosion caused by wind or heavy rains. Their dense foliage acts as a natural barrier, preventing soil particles from being washed away.
2. Weed Suppression: Cover crops compete with weeds for light, water, and nutrients, reducing weed growth in your garden. They act as living mulch, shading the soil surface and preventing weed seeds from germinating.
3. Improved Soil Structure: The roots of cover crops penetrate the soil, loosening compacted areas and improving its structure. They enhance the soil's ability to absorb and retain water, reduce runoff, and increase overall drainage.
4. Nutrient Cycling: Cover crops capture and recycle nutrients from deep within the soil, preventing leaching and making them available for future crops. When the cover crop is tilled or cut and left on the soil surface, it decomposes, releasing organic matter and nutrients.
5. Nitrogen Fixation: Certain cover crops, such as legumes (e.g., clover, vetch, or beans), have the unique ability to fix nitrogen from the air and convert it into a form that plants can use. This reduces the need for synthetic fertilizers and improves soil fertility.
6. Crop Rotation Aid: Cover crops fit perfectly into crop rotation plans. By planting different cover crops in rotation, you can disrupt pest and disease cycles, suppress weed growth, and maintain soil health over time.
7. Winter Protection: Winter cover crops protect the soil during the dormant season. They prevent soil erosion, capture nutrients, and provide organic matter that enriches the soil when tilled or incorporated in the spring.

CHAPTER 5 PLANTING

Here's how to grow cover crops effectively:

- Select the Right Cover Crop: Choose cover crops that suit your climate, soil type, and specific goals. Some common options include legumes (nitrogen fixers), grasses, or a mix of both.
- Timing is Key: Plant cover crops after your main crop is harvested or during periods when the garden beds would otherwise be left fallow. Sow cover crop seeds in late summer or early fall to allow them enough time to establish before winter.
- Prepare the Soil: Clear the garden bed of debris and weeds, and loosen the soil using a rake or garden fork. Follow the specific planting instructions for the cover crop you've chosen.
- Planting and Maintenance: Sow the cover crop seeds evenly over the prepared soil, following the recommended spacing and depth. Lightly rake the seeds into the soil, ensuring good seed-to-soil contact. Water gently and keep the soil moist until the cover crop establishes.
- Termination and Incorporation: In spring, before your main crop planting, terminate the cover crop by mowing, tilling, or cutting it close to the ground. Allow the plant material to decompose on the soil surface or incorporate it into the soil to release nutrients.

By incorporating cover crops into your garden, you can improve soil health, reduce weed pressure, and enhance overall productivity. This sustainable practice nurtures the long-term health of your garden while providing multiple benefits for your plants and the environment.

#42 Plant densely: This helps reduce the space for weed growth.
The Dense Planting Hack:

Planting densely is a strategic gardening technique that not only maximizes space utilization but also helps to naturally suppress weed growth. By crowding plants closely together, you create a dense canopy that shades the soil, reducing the available space for weeds to establish and thrive. Here's how to employ this method effectively:

1. Optimize Space Utilization: Planting densely allows you to make the most of your garden space. By reducing the gaps between plants, you can grow more crops, flowers, or herbs in the same area, resulting in higher yields and a more productive garden.
2. Shade the Soil: The dense foliage of closely spaced plants shades the soil, creating a natural mulch that limits the amount of sunlight reaching the ground. Weeds require sunlight to germinate and grow, so shading the soil suppresses their growth and emergence.
3. Minimize Bare Soil: Bare soil is an open invitation for weed seeds to take root. By planting densely, you cover more soil surface, leaving little room for weed seeds to find a spot to sprout. The dense foliage also helps to retain soil moisture, which further inhibits weed seed germination.
4. Companion Planting: Incorporate companion planting techniques to enhance the density of your garden. Pairing compatible plants together can create a dense intermingling of foliage, effectively crowding out weed growth. Additionally, certain companion plants can help deter pests that may harm your crops.
5. Mulch Between Plants: Apply a layer of organic mulch,

such as straw, wood chips, or shredded leaves, between densely planted rows or around individual plants. Mulch further inhibits weed growth by blocking sunlight and suppressing weed seed germination.
6. Regular Maintenance: Monitor your densely planted garden regularly and promptly remove any weeds that manage to emerge. Be vigilant in early detection and swift removal to prevent them from establishing and spreading.
7. Water Carefully: When watering your densely planted garden, be mindful of the moisture needs of each plant. Ensure water reaches the roots without causing excessive pooling or waterlogging, which can create favorable conditions for weed growth.
8. Soil Preparation: Before planting, prepare the soil by removing existing weeds and cultivating it to a fine texture. This helps to minimize weed competition and allows your densely planted crops to establish more easily.

By implementing dense planting techniques, you create a living carpet of plants that efficiently uses garden space while naturally suppressing weed growth. This method not only reduces the need for excessive weeding but also enhances the overall health and productivity of your garden.

#43 Train climbing plants: This helps you manage them better and enhances their visual appeal.
The Climbing Plant Training Hack:
Training climbing plants is a smart gardening technique that maximizes space, enhances plant health, and creates an organized and visually appealing garden. By providing support and guidance, you can direct the growth of climbing plants,

encourage efficient use of vertical space, and showcase their beauty. Here's how to train climbing plants effectively:

1. Select the Right Support Structure: Choose a suitable support structure based on the type and growth habit of the climbing plant. Options include trellises, arbors, stakes, or wires attached to walls or fences. Ensure the support is sturdy and can handle the weight and growth of the plant.
2. Plant Near the Support Structure: Position the climbing plant near the support structure when planting. This allows the plant to establish its root system close to the support and simplifies training later on.
3. Identify the Main Stem or Vine: Determine the main stem or vine of the climbing plant. This is the central structure that will serve as the main support for the plant's growth.
4. Gentle Initial Guidance: As the plant grows, gently guide the main stem or vine toward the support structure. Avoid twisting or damaging the plant during the process. Use soft ties, twine, or plant clips to secure the stem to the support structure, allowing it to grow vertically.
5. Encourage Side Shoots: Once the main stem is secured, encourage the growth of side shoots or branches by tying them to the support structure. This helps to create a fuller, more robust plant and maximizes flowering or fruiting potential.
6. Regular Pruning and Trimming: Prune or trim any excessive growth, especially if it deviates from the desired shape or size. Removing overcrowded or weak branches allows the plant to focus its energy on healthy growth and prevents a tangled mess.

CHAPTER 5 PLANTING

7. Regular Maintenance and Adjustments: Monitor the growth of the climbing plant regularly and make necessary adjustments as it grows. Check for any loose or damaged ties, reposition stems if needed, and ensure the plant is adequately supported as it matures.
8. Consider Training Techniques: Explore different training techniques based on the plant's growth habit. For twining plants like clematis or morning glories, guide the tendrils around the support structure. For climbing roses or vining vegetables, tie the stems securely to the support structure at regular intervals.
9. Prune and Train Annually: Perform annual pruning and training during the dormant season or as recommended for each specific plant. This helps maintain the desired shape, controls size, and promotes healthier growth in subsequent seasons.
10. Enjoy the Display: As the climbing plant grows and matures, step back and enjoy the beautiful display it creates. Admire the lush foliage, cascading blooms, or bountiful harvests made possible through proper training and care.

By training climbing plants, you can make the most of your garden's vertical space, showcase their beauty, and create an organized and stunning landscape. With a little guidance and maintenance, your climbing plants will flourish and become the star attractions of your garden.

#44 Group similar plants together: Grouping plants with similar watering and sunlight needs together makes care easier.
The Plant Grouping Hack:
Grouping similar plants together in your garden is a smart

and efficient gardening technique that offers several advantages. By clustering plants with similar needs and characteristics, you can create a visually cohesive garden, simplify maintenance tasks, and promote healthier growth. Here's how to make the most of this strategy:

1. Efficient Resource Allocation: Grouping plants with similar water, light, and nutrient requirements allows you to allocate resources more efficiently. Plants in the same group can share irrigation needs, sunlight exposure, and receive appropriate fertilization, leading to healthier growth and optimal resource utilization.
2. Ease of Maintenance: When plants with similar needs are grouped together, maintenance tasks become more streamlined. You can water, fertilize, and tend to them as a cohesive unit, saving time and effort. This also helps to prevent overwatering or over-fertilizing certain plants and neglecting others.
3. Enhanced Aesthetic Appeal: Grouping plants with similar colors, textures, or growth habits creates visual harmony in your garden. The cohesive arrangement of similar plants can have a striking impact, whether you're creating color-themed areas or showcasing a particular plant type.
4. Efficient Pest and Disease Management: When similar plants are grouped together, it becomes easier to monitor and address pest or disease issues. You can identify common problems more readily and take preventive or corrective measures promptly. This focused approach also minimizes the spread of pests or diseases to other plant groups.
5. Pollination and Cross-Pollination: Grouping plants that

require cross-pollination or specific pollinators together enhances their chances of successful pollination. Bees, butterflies, or other pollinators can easily navigate between the plants, increasing the likelihood of fruit set and a higher yield.

6. Companion Planting Synergies: Grouping companion plants together creates synergistic relationships that benefit both plants. For example, planting aromatic herbs near vegetables can deter pests, or placing nitrogen-fixing legumes near nutrient-demanding crops can enrich the soil. Research companion planting techniques to identify suitable plant combinations.
7. Seasonal Succession: Grouping plants with similar seasonal preferences allows for efficient crop rotation and succession planting. You can replant a particular group with a new crop once the previous one is harvested, ensuring a continuous supply of fresh produce throughout the season.
8. Microclimate Creation: Grouping plants closely together can create a microclimate that helps moderate temperature, retain moisture, and reduce wind impact. This microclimate fosters better growth and protects plants from harsh weather conditions.
9. Ease of Harvest: When plants with similar harvest times are grouped together, harvesting becomes more efficient. You can easily access and collect ripe produce, reducing the chances of missing or damaging fruits or vegetables.
10. Learn and Experiment: Grouping similar plants together allows you to observe their growth habits, respond to their needs, and learn from the results. You can experiment with different techniques, compare performance, and

fine-tune your gardening practices based on the shared characteristics of the grouped plants.

By grouping similar plants together, you can create a well-organized and visually appealing garden, streamline maintenance tasks, and optimize plant health. This approach enhances efficiency, promotes successful growth, and allows you to fully enjoy the beauty and productivity of your garden.

#45 Practice intercropping: Growing certain plants together can save space, repel pests, and enhance growth.

The Intercropping Hack:

Intercropping is a strategic gardening technique where different crops are grown together in the same space to maximize productivity, enhance resource utilization, and create a balanced ecosystem. By interplanting complementary crops, you can maximize yields, deter pests, and promote overall garden health. Here's how to make the most of intercropping in your garden:

1. Complementary Crop Pairing: Select crops that have complementary growth habits, root structures, nutrient requirements, and pest-deterrent properties. Some common intercropping combinations include planting tall crops (e.g., corn) alongside low-growing crops (e.g., lettuce), or growing aromatic herbs near susceptible vegetables to repel pests.
2. Space Optimization: Intercropping allows you to optimize space by growing multiple crops in the same area. Utilize vertical space by planting climbers like beans or cucumbers alongside shorter plants. Fill gaps between larger

plants with quick-growing crops like radishes or salad greens.
3. Enhanced Nutrient Utilization: Planting different crops together improves nutrient utilization and reduces nutrient competition. Combining crops with varying nutrient needs helps prevent depletion of specific elements from the soil. For example, nitrogen-fixing legumes (e.g., peas or beans) enrich the soil with nitrogen, benefiting neighboring plants.
4. Weed Suppression: Intercropping creates a dense and diverse canopy, reducing available space for weeds to establish and grow. The competing crops shade the soil, limiting weed germination and growth. This natural weed suppression can significantly reduce the need for manual weeding.
5. Pest Control: Certain intercropping combinations can help deter pests. For example, planting aromatic herbs like basil or marigold near susceptible crops can repel pests with their strong scents. Combining crops with different growth habits can also disrupt pest life cycles or confuse them with mixed plantings.
6. Improved Pollination: Intercropping can enhance pollination by attracting a diverse range of pollinators. Flowers from different crops provide varied nectar sources, attracting bees, butterflies, and other beneficial insects that aid in pollination. This increases fruit set and improves overall yield.
7. Succession Planting and Crop Rotation: Intercropping facilitates succession planting and crop rotation. As one crop is harvested, another can be planted in its place, ensuring a continuous supply of fresh produce throughout

the season. Rotating crops within intercropped areas helps break pest and disease cycles and maintains soil health.
8. Water and Resource Efficiency: Intercropping optimizes water and resource utilization. Different crops have varied water requirements, and by interplanting, you can efficiently irrigate based on individual needs. Additionally, intercropping can promote microclimates, providing shade and reducing water evaporation.
9. Observation and Learning: Intercropping offers an opportunity to observe plant interactions, growth habits, and productivity. Learn from these observations to refine your intercropping combinations and techniques, tailoring them to your specific garden conditions and goals.
10. Record Keeping: Maintain records of your intercropping combinations and their outcomes. Keep track of which combinations work well together, observe the effects on yields and pest control, and note any lessons learned for future seasons.

By practicing intercropping, you can maximize garden productivity, reduce pests, improve resource utilization, and create a more resilient and diverse ecosystem. Embrace the benefits of intercropping to create a harmonious and bountiful garden that thrives on plant diversity and cooperation.

7

Chapter 6 Water

#46 Regular watering: Most plants prefer consistent moisture. Avoid overwatering as it may cause root rot.

The Regular Watering Hack:

Regular and consistent watering is vital for the health and vitality of your plants. Adequate moisture promotes robust growth, prevents stress, and helps plants reach their full potential. By following this watering hack, you can ensure your plants receive the right amount of water at the right time:

1. Observe and Assess: Monitor your plants regularly to determine their watering needs. Look for signs of wilting, dry soil, or drooping leaves, as these indicate that the plants require water. Additionally, consider environmental factors such as temperature, wind, and sunlight intensity, as they affect water requirements.
2. Water Deeply: When watering, aim to moisten the soil deeply. Shallow watering leads to shallow root growth, making plants more susceptible to stress and drought.

Apply water directly to the base of the plants, allowing it to soak in deeply and encourage roots to grow downwards.
3. Water in the Morning: Watering in the morning is ideal, as it allows plants to absorb moisture before the heat of the day. This ensures that leaves dry off quickly, reducing the risk of fungal diseases. Morning watering also provides plants with the necessary hydration to endure hot afternoons.
4. Mulch to Retain Moisture: Apply a layer of organic mulch, such as wood chips, straw, or shredded leaves, around your plants. Mulch helps to conserve soil moisture by reducing evaporation, suppressing weed growth, and regulating soil temperature.
5. Water at the Root Zone: Direct your watering efforts towards the root zone of the plants. Avoid overhead watering whenever possible, as it can promote the spread of diseases and waste water through evaporation. Instead, use drip irrigation, soaker hoses, or watering cans to deliver water directly to the soil.
6. Establish a Schedule: Develop a watering schedule based on the specific needs of your plants, taking into account their water requirements and the prevailing weather conditions. Adjust the frequency and duration of watering as needed throughout the growing season.
7. Use the Finger Test: Before watering, use the finger test to check soil moisture levels. Insert your finger about an inch deep into the soil near the base of the plant. If it feels dry at this depth, it's time to water. If it's still moist, hold off on watering to prevent over-saturation.
8. Avoid Waterlogging: Overwatering can be as harmful as underwatering. Ensure proper drainage in your garden

beds or containers to prevent waterlogging and root rot. If soil becomes waterlogged, provide additional drainage by creating channels or using raised beds.
9. Water Newly Planted Seedlings: Newly planted seedlings require careful attention to establish strong root systems. Water them gently and frequently to keep the soil consistently moist but not waterlogged. Gradually reduce the frequency as the seedlings grow and develop.
10. Consistency is Key: Consistency in watering is essential for plant health. Avoid erratic watering schedules, as this can stress plants and lead to issues such as blossom end rot, split fruits, or stunted growth. Regular, consistent watering provides plants with a stable and optimal growing environment.

By incorporating regular watering practices into your gardening routine, you can ensure healthy and thriving plants. Consistent moisture levels contribute to vigorous growth, strong root development, and increased overall plant resilience. With a little attention and care, you'll create an environment where your plants can flourish and reach their full potential.

#47 Water at the right time: Watering in the early morning or late evening reduces evaporation.
The Timely Watering Hack:
Watering at the right time is crucial for ensuring efficient water usage, promoting healthy plant growth, and minimizing water stress. By following this watering hack, you can maximize the benefits of watering at the appropriate times:

1. Morning Watering: Water your plants in the early morn-

ing, ideally before the sun is at its peak. Morning watering allows plants to absorb moisture and nutrients when they need them the most. It also gives leaves ample time to dry off before evening, reducing the risk of fungal diseases.

2. Avoid Midday Watering: Avoid watering during the hottest part of the day, typically from late morning to early afternoon. The intense heat causes rapid evaporation, meaning water may not reach the roots effectively. Additionally, water droplets on leaves can act as magnifying lenses, intensifying sunlight and potentially causing leaf burn.

3. Evening Watering: If morning watering is not possible, consider watering in the early evening. This allows plants to uptake moisture before nighttime and helps cool them down after a hot day. However, ensure leaves have enough time to dry off before the onset of cooler nighttime temperatures to prevent fungal issues.

4. Assess Plant Needs: Observe your plants regularly to assess their water requirements. Pay attention to signs of water stress, such as drooping leaves, wilted appearance, or dry soil. Different plants have varying water needs, so it's essential to be attentive to individual requirements.

5. Soil Moisture Monitoring: Check the moisture level of the soil before watering. Use the finger test by inserting your finger about an inch deep into the soil near the plant's base. If it feels dry at this depth, it's time to water. If it's still moist, hold off on watering to avoid oversaturation.

6. Consider Weather Conditions: Factor in the prevailing weather conditions when deciding on watering times. If it has rained recently or if the forecast predicts rainfall, adjust your watering accordingly. Take advantage of natural precipitation and reduce the need for additional

watering when possible.
7. Water Deeply and Infrequently: When you do water, aim to moisten the soil deeply. Infrequent, deep watering encourages plants to develop deep and robust root systems. Shallow and frequent watering can lead to shallow root growth, making plants more susceptible to stress and drought.
8. Water at the Base: Direct your watering efforts toward the base of the plants, focusing on the root zone. Avoid overhead watering whenever possible, as it can promote the spread of diseases and lead to water waste through evaporation. Drip irrigation, soaker hoses, or watering cans are effective methods for targeted watering.
9. Adjust for Plant Growth Stages: Be mindful of the different growth stages of your plants. Young seedlings and newly transplanted plants may require more frequent watering until their root systems become established. As plants mature, adjust the watering frequency accordingly to meet their changing needs.
10. Mulch to Retain Moisture: Apply a layer of organic mulch around your plants to conserve soil moisture. Mulch helps to reduce evaporation, regulate soil temperature, and suppress weed growth. This, in turn, minimizes water loss and helps maintain optimal soil moisture levels.

By watering at the right time, you can optimize water usage, promote healthy plant growth, and minimize water stress in your garden. Timely watering ensures plants receive the necessary moisture when they need it most, contributing to their overall health, vigor, and productivity.

#48 Install a drip irrigation system: This is a water-efficient way to keep your plants hydrated.

The Drip Irrigation Hack:

A drip irrigation system is a highly efficient and water-saving method of watering your garden. It delivers water directly to the root zone of plants, reducing water waste, minimizing evaporation, and promoting healthier plant growth. Here's how to make the most of a drip irrigation system in your garden:

1. Water Efficiency: Drip irrigation systems are highly water-efficient because they deliver water directly to the plants' root zones, reducing evaporation and runoff. They can save up to 50% more water compared to traditional watering methods like sprinklers.
2. Customizable Layout: Drip irrigation systems are customizable to fit the layout of your garden. You can adjust the placement, spacing, and flow rate of the emitters to meet the specific needs of each plant or garden area.
3. Consistent Watering: Drip irrigation provides consistent and uniform watering, ensuring each plant receives the right amount of water. It eliminates overwatering or underwatering that can occur with other watering methods.
4. Reduced Weed Growth: Drip irrigation delivers water directly to the root zone of plants, minimizing water availability to weed seeds. This helps suppress weed growth, reducing competition for nutrients and space in your garden.
5. Healthy Roots: The slow and steady water application of drip irrigation encourages deep root growth. Plants develop strong and extensive root systems, making them more resilient and efficient in absorbing nutrients from

the soil.
6. Reduced Disease Risk: Drip irrigation minimizes leaf wetness, reducing the risk of fungal diseases that thrive in moist conditions. By avoiding overhead watering, you create a drier environment that is less conducive to disease development.
7. Time and Labor Savings: Once set up, a drip irrigation system requires minimal maintenance and saves you time and effort. It eliminates the need for manual watering, allowing you to focus on other garden tasks or enjoy your leisure time.
8. Easy Installation: Drip irrigation systems are relatively easy to install. Kits and components are readily available, and installation instructions are straightforward. Basic tools and connectors are typically all that's needed to set up the system.
9. Mulch Compatibility: Drip irrigation systems work well with organic mulches. Apply a layer of mulch around plants to conserve soil moisture and further reduce evaporation. The mulch also helps maintain a more even soil temperature.
10. System Monitoring: Regularly inspect and monitor your drip irrigation system to ensure proper functioning. Check for clogged emitters, leaks, or damaged tubing. Flush the system periodically to remove any debris or sediment that may cause blockages.

By implementing a drip irrigation system in your garden, you can conserve water, promote healthier plants, and save time and effort. The precise and efficient delivery of water directly to the root zone ensures your plants receive the moisture they need without waste. Embrace this water-saving technology and enjoy the benefits of a well-maintained and thriving garden.

#49 Collect rainwater: It's a great way to save water, and plants love rainwater.

The Rainwater Collection Hack:

Collecting rainwater is a sustainable and cost-effective way to provide your garden with a natural water source. It helps conserve water, reduce water bills, and ensures a consistent supply of water for your plants. Here's how to make the most of rainwater collection in your garden:

1. Choose a Rain Barrel or Container: Select a rain barrel or container that suits your garden size and needs. Look for options with a tight-fitting lid or mesh screen to prevent debris, insects, and mosquitoes from entering the water.
2. Positioning and Placement: Place your rain barrel or container beneath a downspout or gutter to collect rainwater directly from your roof. Ensure it is on a stable surface and positioned near your garden for convenient access.
3. Rainwater Diversion: Attach a diverter or downspout extension to direct rainwater into the barrel or container. This helps maximize the collection efficiency and prevents water overflow during heavy rainfall.
4. Maintenance and Cleaning: Regularly inspect and clean your rain barrel or container to keep the water free from debris and prevent stagnation. Clean the gutter or downspout system to avoid blockages that can hinder water flow.
5. Use a Filter System: Consider using a filter system to remove larger debris and sediment from the collected

rainwater. This helps prevent clogging in watering cans, hoses, or drip irrigation systems when using the collected water.

6. Watering Can Access: Position your rain barrel at a suitable height or use a rain barrel stand to allow easy access for filling watering cans. This eliminates the need for additional pumping or transferring of water.
7. Optimal Water Utilization: Use rainwater for various gardening purposes such as watering plants, washing gardening tools, or cleaning outdoor surfaces. Rainwater is free from chlorine and other chemicals, making it ideal for sensitive plants.
8. Supplement During Dry Spells: During periods of prolonged drought or limited rainfall, use rainwater as a supplement to your regular watering routine. Combine rainwater with other water sources to ensure sufficient hydration for your plants.
9. Overflow Utilization: Direct overflow from your rain barrel to permeable areas in your garden, such as flower beds or vegetable patches. This allows excess water to be absorbed by the soil, replenishing groundwater and preventing water pooling.
10. Educate and Advocate: Share your rainwater collection practices with others and promote the importance of water conservation. Encourage your community or neighbors to embrace rainwater collection to collectively contribute to a more sustainable water future.

By collecting rainwater, you can reduce water consumption, lower your water bills, and provide your garden with a natural and environmentally friendly water source. Embrace rainwater harvesting as an effective way to conserve resources and nurture your plants, while promoting sustainable gardening practices.

#50 Recycle water: Use cooking water or aquarium water to water your plants. They contain nutrients beneficial for plants.

The Water Recycling Hack:

Recycling water from cooking or aquariums is a sustainable gardening practice that conserves water and reduces waste. By repurposing water that would otherwise be discarded, you can provide your plants with a nutrient-rich and eco-friendly water source. Here's how to make the most of water recycling in your garden:

1. Cooking Water: After cooking vegetables, pasta, or boiling eggs, allow the water to cool before recycling it in your garden. The nutrient content in the cooking water can benefit your plants, providing them with valuable minerals and organic matter.
2. Natural Cooling Process: Before using cooking water, ensure it has cooled to room temperature or is lukewarm. Avoid using extremely hot or boiling water, as it may harm delicate plant roots or create temperature extremes in the soil.
3. No Salt or Seasonings: Use cooking water that does not contain excessive salt, spices, or seasonings. These additives can potentially harm plants or disrupt the balance of nutrients in the soil. Plain water from boiling or steaming is best for recycling.
4. Aquarium Water: When cleaning your aquarium, save the water rather than disposing of it. The water from

aquariums contains beneficial nutrients and minerals that can enhance plant growth.
5. Non-Toxic and Chemical-Free: Ensure the water from your aquarium is free from any harmful chemicals, medications, or additives that may be detrimental to plants. Avoid using water that has been treated with medications or chemicals harmful to plant life.
6. Watering Application: Use recycled water from cooking or aquariums to water non-edible plants, flowers, or ornamental plants in your garden. This ensures that any potential contaminants or additives do not come into contact with edible produce.
7. Moderation and Balance: While recycled water can benefit plants, it is important to use it in moderation and in balance with regular watering. Alternate the use of recycled water with fresh water to prevent nutrient imbalances or excess build-up in the soil.
8. Avoid Overwatering: Ensure that recycled water does not contribute to overwatering your plants. Test the soil moisture level before watering, and adjust the amount of recycled water used accordingly. Remember, plants still require appropriate drainage and drying periods to thrive.
9. Composting Potential: Consider using cooking water that contains vegetable scraps or mild organic matter as a liquid addition to your compost pile. The nutrients and organic content in the water can enhance the decomposition process and contribute to nutrient-rich compost.
10. Educate and Raise Awareness: Share your water recycling practices with others to encourage sustainable gardening and water conservation. Help spread the message about

the benefits of recycling water, reducing waste, and promoting eco-friendly gardening practices.

By recycling water from cooking or aquariums, you can minimize water waste, conserve resources, and provide your plants with a supplementary source of nutrients. Embrace water recycling as an eco-conscious gardening practice, contributing to a more sustainable and resilient garden ecosystem.

#51 Use milk jugs to water plants: Poke holes in the cap for a slow release watering system.
The Milk Jug Watering Hack:
Using milk jugs as a self-watering system is a clever and cost-effective way to provide a steady water supply to your plants, especially in areas with limited rainfall or during periods of drought. By repurposing milk jugs, you can create a DIY irrigation system that helps keep your plants hydrated. Here's how to make the most of milk jugs for watering your plants:

1. Prepare the Milk Jug: Rinse out a plastic milk jug thoroughly to remove any milk residue. Remove the cap and make a small hole in the lid using a nail or a small drill bit. This hole will allow water to slowly drip out, ensuring a steady and controlled flow.
2. Fill the Milk Jug: Fill the milk jug with water, leaving a small airspace at the top to prevent overflow when the water expands due to temperature changes. Securely screw the lid back on, making sure the hole is facing downwards.
3. Select the Plant Location: Choose a location near the plant you want to water, ensuring it is within reach of the milk

jug's drip line. Ideally, place the milk jug on higher ground or elevate it using a brick or sturdy platform to facilitate gravity-fed watering.
4. Dig a Hole or Trench: Dig a small hole or trench next to the plant, deep enough to bury the milk jug up to its neck. This hole will allow the water to directly reach the root zone of the plant, promoting efficient absorption and reducing water loss.
5. Plant the Milk Jug: Place the milk jug in the hole, ensuring the lid is facing downwards and the hole in the lid is exposed. Gently backfill the hole or trench with soil, firmly securing the milk jug in place while allowing water to drip out through the hole in the lid.
6. Monitor and Adjust: Monitor the water level in the milk jug regularly and refill it as needed. Depending on the plant's water requirements and environmental conditions, you may need to adjust the frequency of refilling the milk jug.
7. Mulch and Protect: Apply a layer of organic mulch around the base of the plant and over the area where the milk jug is buried. Mulch helps conserve moisture, reduces evaporation, and protects the soil from temperature extremes.
8. Experiment and Adapt: Depending on the specific needs of your plants and the rate of water absorption, you can modify the size of the hole in the milk jug's lid to control the flow rate. Experiment with different hole sizes to achieve the desired watering rate.
9. Benefit from Consistent Watering: The self-watering system created by the milk jug ensures a consistent supply of water to your plants, helping to prevent underwatering or overwatering. This method is particularly useful during hot summer months or when you're away for extended

periods.

10. Reuse and Recycle: As the milk jug watering system becomes empty, refill it as needed and continue using it throughout the growing season. At the end of the season, rinse out the milk jug and store it for future use or recycle it responsibly.

By repurposing milk jugs as self-watering devices, you can provide your plants with a reliable water source while conserving water and reducing manual watering efforts. This simple DIY hack helps maintain plant health and vitality, particularly during challenging environmental conditions.

#52 Use a wine bottle to water plants: Fill with water and turn upside down into the soil for a slow-release watering method.

The Wine Bottle Watering Hack:

Repurposing wine bottles as a slow-release watering system is an innovative and sustainable way to keep your plants hydrated, especially when you're away or during dry periods. By using wine bottles, you can create an efficient and self-regulating watering method. Here's how to make the most of wine bottles for watering your plants:

1. Select Suitable Wine Bottles: Choose wine bottles with cork or screw-top lids. Clear or colored glass bottles work equally well. Ensure the bottles are thoroughly cleaned and rinsed to remove any wine residue.
2. Prepare the Wine Bottle: Remove any labels or adhesive from the wine bottle. Wash the bottle with warm soapy water and rinse it thoroughly. Allow the bottle to dry completely before proceeding.

3. Pierce Holes in the Cork or Lid: If using a cork, drill or poke several small holes through the cork using a small nail or drill bit. If using a screw-top lid, drill or create a small opening in the center using a drill bit or heated metal object.
4. Moisten the Soil: Before inserting the wine bottle into the soil, ensure the plant's root zone is adequately moist. This helps establish proper capillary action and ensures water absorption from the bottle.
5. Dig a Hole: Dig a small hole near the base of the plant, deep enough to bury the wine bottle up to the neck. The hole should be wide enough to accommodate the wine bottle without causing damage to the plant's roots.
6. Insert the Wine Bottle: Insert the wine bottle into the hole, cork or lid side down, leaving a few inches of the neck above the soil surface. Ensure the holes in the cork or lid are exposed and facing downward.
7. Backfill and Secure: Carefully backfill the hole with soil, ensuring the wine bottle remains upright and stable. Pack the soil firmly around the bottle to secure it in place and prevent it from tilting or being dislodged.
8. Monitor and Refill: Monitor the water level in the wine bottle regularly and refill it as needed. Depending on the size of the bottle and the plant's water requirements, you may need to adjust the frequency of refilling.
9. Mulch and Protect: Apply a layer of organic mulch around the base of the plant and over the area where the wine bottle is buried. Mulch helps conserve moisture, suppress weed growth, and protect the soil from temperature fluctuations.
10. Reuse and Adapt: Empty and rinse the wine bottle as

needed, refilling it with water and reinserting it into the soil. Experiment with different bottle sizes, hole sizes in the cork or lid, or placement in the garden to best suit the water needs of different plants.

By repurposing wine bottles as slow-release watering devices, you can provide your plants with a steady water supply, especially during periods of low rainfall or when you're away. This DIY hack helps maintain plant health, conserves water, and reduces the need for frequent manual watering. Cheers to an innovative and sustainable way of keeping your plants hydrated!

8

Chapter 7 Compost and Mulch

#53 Use compost: Compost enriches the soil, provides nutrients for the plants, and helps retain water.

The Compost Gardening Hack:

Utilizing compost in your garden is a powerful way to improve soil fertility, enhance plant growth, and reduce waste. Compost is a nutrient-rich, organic matter that replenishes soil with essential elements, improves soil structure, and promotes overall garden health. Here's how to make the most of compost in your garden:

1. Start Your Own Compost: Begin composting at home by collecting kitchen scraps, yard waste, and other organic materials. Compost bins or piles can be set up in your garden or even in small spaces like balconies or patios. Turn the compost regularly to speed up the decomposition process.
2. Balance Compost Ingredients: Maintain a balanced mix of green and brown materials in your compost. Greens include kitchen scraps, grass clippings, and fresh plant trimmings. Browns include dry leaves, straw, and woody materials. The proper balance ensures optimal decomposition and nutrient content in the compost.
3. Aim for Proper Moisture and Aeration: Keep your compost pile moist, similar to a wrung-out sponge. Ensure proper aeration by turning the pile regularly or using a compost aerator tool. Well-aerated compost decomposes faster and prevents foul odors or anaerobic conditions.
4. Screen the Finished Compost: Once the compost has broken down into a dark, crumbly material, screen it to remove any large debris or clumps. This screened compost is ready for use in the garden, providing a nutrient-rich amendment to improve soil quality.
5. Incorporate Compost into Soil: Prior to planting, incorporate compost into the soil. Spread a layer of compost over the garden beds or mix it thoroughly with existing soil. This enriches the soil with organic matter, improves

CHAPTER 7 COMPOST AND MULCH

soil structure, and enhances its ability to retain moisture and nutrients.
6. Top-Dress Existing Plants: Apply a thin layer of compost around the base of established plants. This top-dressing provides a slow-release source of nutrients and organic matter, feeding the plants over time and improving soil health.
7. Mulch with Compost: Use compost as a mulch layer around plants to suppress weeds, retain moisture, and provide a continuous supply of nutrients as it slowly breaks down. Apply a layer of compost mulch, leaving space around the plant's stem to prevent moisture-related issues.
8. Compost Tea: Create compost tea by steeping compost in water and straining out the solids. Use the resulting liquid to water your plants or apply it as a foliar spray. Compost tea provides an immediate boost of nutrients and beneficial microorganisms to support plant growth.
9. Compost for Seed Starting: Create a potting mix for seed starting by combining compost with other soilless mediums like vermiculite or perlite. This provides young seedlings with a nutrient-rich environment, promoting healthy growth from the start.
10. Continuous Composting: Maintain a continuous composting process by adding new organic materials regularly and turning the compost pile as needed. By ensuring a steady supply of compost, you can consistently enrich your garden soil and reap its numerous benefits.

By incorporating compost into your gardening routine, you can improve soil fertility, increase plant vigor, and reduce the need for synthetic fertilizers. Compost enriches the soil with nutrients, enhances soil structure, and promotes a thriving garden ecosystem. Embrace the power of composting to create a sustainable and vibrant garden that thrives with organic abundance.

#54 Mulch: Mulching reduces weed growth and helps the soil retain moisture.

The Mulching Gardening Hack:

Using mulch in your garden is a simple yet effective technique that provides numerous benefits. Mulch helps conserve moisture, suppress weeds, regulate soil temperature, and improve overall soil health. Here's how to make the most of mulch in your garden:

1. Choose the Right Mulch: Select a suitable mulch material based on your garden's needs and the plants you're growing. Common options include organic mulches like wood chips, straw, shredded leaves, or compost, as well as inorganic mulches like gravel or landscape fabric.
2. Apply the Correct Thickness: Apply a layer of mulch with the appropriate thickness. For organic mulches, aim for a depth of 2 to 4 inches, while inorganic mulches require a thinner layer. Avoid piling mulch against plant stems or tree trunks, as it can create a moist environment that promotes rot or disease.
3. Mulch When Soil is Moist: Apply mulch when the soil is slightly moist to help lock in moisture and create a more effective barrier against evaporation. Avoid mulching over dry soil, as it can prevent water penetration and hinder plant growth.

4. **Mulch After Weeding:** Remove any existing weeds before applying mulch to your garden beds. Weeds left under the mulch can continue to grow and compete with your plants for resources. Take the time to weed thoroughly, and then apply mulch to suppress future weed growth.
5. **Leave Space Around Plant Stems:** Create a slight gap around the base of plants or tree trunks to prevent moisture buildup and potential rot. Avoid piling mulch directly against plant stems, allowing proper airflow and reducing the risk of pests and diseases.
6. **Utilize Mulch as a Weed Barrier:** A thick layer of mulch acts as a natural weed barrier, preventing weed seeds from germinating and competing with your plants. This reduces the need for manual weeding and conserves moisture, creating a more efficient and low-maintenance garden.
7. **Regulate Soil Temperature:** Mulch acts as insulation, moderating soil temperature by keeping it cooler in hot weather and warmer during colder periods. This helps protect plant roots from extreme temperature fluctuations and creates a more stable growing environment.
8. **Conserve Moisture:** Mulch helps conserve soil moisture by reducing evaporation. It acts as a protective layer, shielding the soil from direct sunlight and wind exposure. This allows your plants to access the water they need while reducing the frequency of watering.
9. **Improve Soil Health:** Organic mulches gradually break down, enriching the soil with organic matter and nutrients. As the mulch decomposes, it improves soil structure, enhances microbial activity, and promotes a healthy soil ecosystem for optimal plant growth.

10. **Top-Dress Mulch Annually:** Replenish mulch annually or as needed, as it will naturally break down over time. Adding a fresh layer of mulch helps maintain its effectiveness in conserving moisture, suppressing weeds, and improving overall soil health.

By incorporating mulch in your garden, you can conserve water, reduce weed growth, regulate soil temperature, and improve the overall health of your plants. Embrace the benefits of mulching to create a more resilient and thriving garden that requires less maintenance and fosters optimal plant growth.

#55 Learn to compost: It's great for reducing kitchen waste and improving your soil.

The Kitchen Waste Composting Hack: Turning Scraps into Soil Gold

Do you find yourself throwing away a significant amount of kitchen waste every day? It's time to transform that waste into something valuable for your garden! Composting is a simple and effective way to reduce kitchen waste while creating nutrient-rich soil amendment. Let's explore how you can turn your kitchen scraps into "soil gold" through composting:

1. **Collect and Sort:** Start by setting up a designated container in your kitchen for collecting food scraps. Use a small countertop compost bin or a lidded container to store vegetable peelings, fruit scraps, coffee grounds, tea bags, crushed eggshells, and non-greasy food leftovers. Avoid including meat, dairy, oily products, or cooked food, as they can attract pests or slow down the composting process.

2. Choose a Composting Method: There are several composting methods to suit different situations. If you have a backyard, consider setting up a traditional compost bin or pile. If you're short on space, try vermicomposting with a worm bin indoors or a compost tumbler on your balcony or patio. Choose a method that fits your needs and available resources.
3. Balance Your Ingredients: Composting is all about balance. Aim for a mix of "greens" and "browns" to create the ideal environment for decomposition. Greens include nitrogen-rich materials like fruit and vegetable scraps, while browns consist of carbon-rich materials such as dry leaves, straw, or shredded paper. Aim for a ratio of roughly 3 parts browns to 1 part greens by volume.
4. Layer and Moisturize: Begin your compost pile by layering greens and browns. Start with a layer of browns, followed by a layer of greens, and continue this alternating pattern. Moisten each layer as you go to ensure proper moisture content. The compost pile should be damp, similar to a well-wrung sponge, but not overly saturated.
5. Aerate and Turn: To encourage decomposition, aerate your compost pile regularly. Use a garden fork or a compost turning tool to mix the materials, introducing oxygen and promoting the breakdown of organic matter. Turning the pile every few weeks helps speed up the composting process and prevents unpleasant odors.
6. Patience and Time: Composting takes time, so be patient. The process can vary from a few months to a year, depending on factors like temperature, moisture, and the size of the materials. Over time, the organic waste will transform into dark, crumbly compost—a testament to your efforts.

7. Use Your Finished Compost: Once your compost is ready, use it to enrich your garden soil. Incorporate it into the planting beds or mix it with potting soil for container gardening. Your homemade compost will improve soil structure, enhance water retention, promote beneficial microbial activity, and provide essential nutrients to your plants.
8. Compost Troubleshooting: If you encounter issues like an unpleasant odor, fruit flies, or slow decomposition, troubleshoot by adjusting the moisture levels, adding more browns for carbon balance, or ensuring proper aeration. Remember, composting is a learning process, and you'll refine your skills over time.

By composting your kitchen waste, you can significantly reduce the amount of organic matter ending up in landfills while creating a valuable resource for your garden. Embrace the power of composting as a way to close the loop, reduce waste, and nourish your plants naturally. Let your kitchen scraps become the foundation of healthy and thriving soil, benefitting both your garden and the environment.

#56 Create a compost heap: It's a good way to recycle kitchen scraps and improve your soil.

The Compost Heap Hack: Transforming Waste into Nutrient-Rich Gold

Creating a compost heap is a fantastic way to turn your organic waste into nutrient-rich compost, nourishing your garden and reducing your environmental impact. With a few simple steps, you can build a compost heap that efficiently breaks down organic materials and produces "black gold" for

CHAPTER 7 COMPOST AND MULCH

your plants. Let's dive in:

1. Select the Right Location: Choose a suitable location for your compost heap. Find a spot that is well-drained, easily accessible, and ideally close to your garden for convenience. Ensure the area receives some sunlight, as this helps with decomposition.
2. Prepare the Base: Clear the area of any grass or weeds to provide a clean base for your compost heap. Consider placing a layer of twigs or straw at the bottom to promote air circulation and drainage.
3. Layer Your Compost: Begin layering your compost heap with a mix of "browns" and "greens." Browns include dry leaves, straw, wood chips, or shredded paper, providing carbon-rich material. Greens consist of fresh grass clippings, vegetable scraps, coffee grounds, or plant trimmings, providing nitrogen-rich material. Alternate between the two layers, starting with a layer of browns.
4. Maintain the Right Moisture Level: Keep your compost heap moist but not waterlogged. It should resemble a damp sponge. If the pile becomes too dry, sprinkle it with water. If it becomes too wet, add more dry materials like leaves or straw to improve air circulation and prevent odors.
5. Provide Adequate Airflow: Oxygen is essential for decomposition. To ensure proper airflow, regularly turn or aerate the compost heap using a pitchfork or garden fork. This helps mix the materials, introduces oxygen, and speeds up the decomposition process.
6. Size Matters: Consider the size of your compost heap. While there's no strict rule, a compost heap should ideally

be at least 3 feet wide, 3 feet deep, and 3 feet high. This size provides the right conditions for decomposition and maintains sufficient heat.
7. Cover the Heap: Covering your compost heap helps retain moisture and heat while preventing excess rain from soaking the pile. You can use a tarp, old carpet, or a layer of straw to cover the top. Ensure the cover is easy to remove when you need to access the compost.
8. Additional Tips: To accelerate decomposition, chop or shred larger materials into smaller pieces. Avoid adding meat, dairy products, oily materials, or diseased plant material to your compost heap, as they can attract pests or promote disease. Keep a small container in your kitchen to collect food scraps and periodically add them to your compost heap.
9. Monitor and Maintain: Regularly check your compost heap's moisture level, temperature, and progress. Aim for a temperature range of 120-160°F (49-71°C) to facilitate decomposition. If needed, adjust the moisture or turn the heap to maintain optimal conditions.
10. Harvest the Compost: Over time, your compost heap will break down into dark, crumbly compost—ready to be used in your garden. Harvest the compost by removing the finished material from the bottom of the heap. The remaining partially decomposed material can be returned to the heap for further breakdown.

With your own compost heap, you'll reduce waste, create nutrient-rich compost, and nurture your plants naturally. Remember to be patient, as composting takes time. As you continue the process, you'll become more familiar with what works best for your compost heap. Enjoy the journey of transforming waste into "black gold."

#57 Mulch your perennial beds: This keeps them weed-free and the soil moist and fertilized.

The Perennial Bed Mulching Hack: Promoting Growth, Suppressing Weeds, and Conserving Moisture

Mulching perennial beds is a smart gardening practice that provides numerous benefits. It helps maintain soil moisture, suppresses weed growth, regulates soil temperature, and adds a finishing touch to your garden's aesthetics. Here's how to make the most of mulching in your perennial beds:

1. Choose the Right Mulch: Select a suitable mulch material for your perennial beds. Organic options include shredded bark, wood chips, straw, or compost. Inorganic options like gravel or pebbles can also be used for certain garden styles. Consider the overall look you want to achieve and the specific needs of your plants.
2. Prepare the Bed: Before applying mulch, prepare your perennial bed by removing any weeds or existing vegetation. It's best to start with a clean slate to prevent weed growth beneath the mulch layer. Take the time to edge the bed neatly for a polished appearance.
3. Mulch Thickness: Apply a layer of mulch with a thickness of 2 to 4 inches. This depth provides ample coverage to suppress weeds, retain moisture, and insulate the soil. Avoid piling mulch against plant stems or trunks, as this can create a moist environment that leads to disease or rot.
4. Water Before Mulching: It's advisable to water the peren-

nial bed thoroughly before applying mulch. Moist soil helps lock in moisture, and the mulch acts as a protective barrier against evaporation, keeping the soil consistently moist for the plants' benefit.

5. Leave Space Around Plants: Create a small gap or "mulch-free zone" around the base of perennial plants to prevent excessive moisture buildup and potential rot. This gap also allows proper airflow and prevents the mulch from directly contacting plant stems, reducing the risk of pests or diseases.
6. Mulch Maintenance: Periodically inspect and refresh the mulch layer as needed. Mulch can break down over time and become thinner, allowing weed growth and reducing its effectiveness. Add a fresh layer of mulch annually or as required to maintain the desired thickness.
7. Consider Compost as Mulch: If you have compost readily available, consider using it as a mulch layer in your perennial beds. Compost acts as a slow-release fertilizer, enriching the soil and providing a nutrient boost to your plants. Apply a thin layer of compost as a top-dressing before adding a traditional mulch layer.
8. Mulching Timing: Apply mulch in the early spring or late fall to maximize its benefits. In the spring, mulch helps conserve soil moisture during the warmer months and suppresses early weed growth. In the fall, it helps insulate the soil, protecting plants' roots from extreme temperatures and providing a tidy appearance during the dormant season.
9. Monitor and Adjust: Keep an eye on your mulched perennial beds throughout the growing season. Adjust the mulch thickness if necessary, especially in areas where

soil erosion or compaction may occur. Be mindful of any signs of excessive moisture, such as waterlogged soil or fungal issues, and adjust the mulch accordingly.
10. Enjoy the Benefits: Embrace the advantages of mulching your perennial beds. Not only does it improve the overall appearance of your garden, but it also conserves moisture, suppresses weeds, and provides insulation to promote healthier and more vibrant perennial plants.

By mulching your perennial beds, you create a nurturing environment for your plants, reduce maintenance efforts, and enhance the overall beauty of your garden. Embrace the practice of mulching and reap the rewards of healthier, more resilient perennial beds year after year.

#58 Use tea and coffee grounds: They acidify the soil, great for acid-loving plants.
The Tea and Coffee Grounds Mulching Hack: Boosting Soil Health and Plant Growth
Tea and coffee grounds aren't just for sipping—they can also be a valuable resource in your garden! Using them as mulch provides numerous benefits, such as adding organic matter to the soil, enhancing soil fertility, and promoting healthy plant growth. Here's how to make the most of tea and coffee grounds as mulch:

1. Collect Used Tea and Coffee Grounds: Start by collecting your used tea bags or loose tea leaves and coffee grounds. Allow them to cool and dry before using them as mulch. Accumulate a sufficient amount to cover the desired area in your garden.

2. Prepare the Garden Bed: Before applying tea and coffee grounds as mulch, prepare the garden bed by removing any existing weeds or debris. This provides a clean surface for the mulch and reduces competition for nutrients with unwanted plants.
3. Mix with Other Organic Mulch Materials: Tea and coffee grounds work best when combined with other organic mulch materials. Consider mixing them with dry leaves, straw, wood chips, or compost to provide a well-balanced and diverse mulch layer. This combination improves soil structure, retains moisture, and encourages beneficial microbial activity.
4. Apply the Mulch: Spread a thin layer of the tea and coffee ground mixture evenly over the garden bed. Aim for a layer thickness of about 1 to 2 inches. Avoid piling the mulch directly against plant stems or trunks, as this can create a moist environment that promotes rot or disease. Leave a small gap around the base of plants to allow for proper airflow.
5. Mulch Maintenance: Regularly monitor the mulch layer and replenish it as needed. Over time, the mulch will break down and decompose, so adding fresh materials periodically helps maintain an effective mulch layer. Also, periodically mix the mulch into the soil to prevent compaction and promote nutrient distribution.
6. Consider Composting: If you have a compost pile, consider adding used tea bags and coffee grounds to your composting efforts. They provide valuable organic matter and nutrients to the compost, enhancing its quality. Once fully decomposed, the compost can be used as a nutrient-rich soil amendment or incorporated into your garden

CHAPTER 7 COMPOST AND MULCH

beds.

7. Avoid Overuse: While tea and coffee grounds are beneficial, it's important to avoid overusing them as mulch. Aim for a balanced approach by combining them with other organic materials. This helps prevent excessive acidity in the soil, which could negatively affect certain plants.
8. Benefit Acid-Loving Plants: Tea and coffee grounds have a slightly acidic pH, making them excellent mulch choices for acid-loving plants such as azaleas, rhododendrons, hydrangeas, and blueberries. These plants thrive in slightly acidic soil, and the tea and coffee grounds can help maintain their preferred pH levels.
9. Enjoy Pest-Repelling Properties: Tea and coffee grounds can act as a natural deterrent to certain garden pests. Slugs, snails, and even cats dislike the texture and smell of coffee grounds, making them less likely to venture into mulched areas. This can help protect your plants and keep unwanted critters at bay.
10. Observe and Adjust: Monitor the response of your plants to the tea and coffee grounds mulch. Some plants may benefit more than others, so observe their growth and health. If you notice any adverse effects or signs of over-acidity, adjust the amount or frequency of using tea and coffee grounds as mulch.

By utilizing tea and coffee grounds as mulch, you can enhance soil health, promote plant growth, and reduce waste from your daily beverages. Embrace the sustainability and benefits of repurposing these kitchen scraps to create an organic and nutrient-rich environment for your garden. Sip your tea or coffee, then let their grounds work their magic in your mulched beds!

#59 Make your own compost tea: Soak compost in water and use the water as a nutrient-rich plant feed.

The DIY Compost Tea Hack: Nourishing Plants with Liquid Gold

Compost tea is like a supercharged elixir for your plants, packed with nutrients and beneficial microorganisms. Making your own compost tea is an excellent way to amplify the benefits of compost and provide your plants with a nutrient-rich boost. Here's how to create your own liquid gold:

1. Gather Your Materials: Start by gathering the necessary materials. You'll need compost, a large container (such as a bucket or a garbage can), water, an aerator or air stone, a pump, and a mesh bag or old pillowcase to hold the compost.
2. Select Quality Compost: Choose well-aged, finished compost for your compost tea. This mature compost is rich in nutrients and contains a diverse community of beneficial microorganisms that will enrich your tea.
3. Prepare the Compost Tea Bag: Fill the mesh bag or pillowcase with a generous amount of compost. Tie it securely, ensuring that the compost is enclosed and won't escape during the brewing process.
4. Fill the Container with Water: Fill the container with water, ideally chlorine-free water like rainwater or well water. If tap water is your only option, let it sit out for 24 hours to allow any chlorine to evaporate.
5. Submerge the Compost Tea Bag: Immerse the compost tea bag in the water, ensuring it is fully submerged. Attach

the aerator or air stone to the pump and place it in the container. The aerator will oxygenate the water, creating an ideal environment for the microorganisms to thrive.
6. Brewing Time: Let the compost tea steep for 24 to 48 hours, stirring occasionally. The microorganisms from the compost will multiply and release beneficial enzymes and nutrients into the water, creating a potent brew.
7. Strain and Apply: After the brewing period, remove the compost tea bag from the container. Strain the tea to remove any remaining solids, using a fine mesh strainer or cheesecloth. The strained liquid is now your homemade compost tea, ready to be applied to your plants.
8. Apply the Compost Tea: Dilute the compost tea with water at a ratio of approximately 1:10 (1 part compost tea to 10 parts water). Pour or spray the diluted compost tea onto the soil around the base of your plants. Ensure thorough coverage, as the tea will deliver nutrients and beneficial microorganisms directly to the roots.
9. Timing and Frequency: Apply compost tea during the growing season, preferably in the early morning or late afternoon to minimize evaporation. For established plants, apply every two to three weeks. For seedlings or young plants, apply more sparingly, once every four to six weeks.
10. Clean and Repeat: Clean your container and equipment thoroughly after each use to prevent the growth of harmful pathogens or algae. Then, start another batch of compost tea to continue nourishing your plants throughout the growing season.

By making your own compost tea, you can maximize the benefits of compost and provide your plants with a potent source of nutrients and beneficial microorganisms. This homemade elixir will contribute to healthier plants, increased disease resistance, improved soil fertility, and overall garden vitality. Cheers to creating your own liquid gold and witnessing the remarkable impact it has on your plants!

Chapter 8 Fertilizers

#60 Use natural fertilizers: They release nutrients more slowly than synthetic ones and improve your soil's ability to hold water.

The Natural Fertilizers Hack: Nourishing Your Garden with Organic Power

When it comes to fertilizing your garden, nature has already provided you with a treasure trove of organic options. Natural fertilizers are not only effective but also environmentally friendly, helping you cultivate a thriving garden without the use of synthetic chemicals. Here's how to harness the power of natural fertilizers:

1. Compost - The Gardener's Gold: Compost is the cornerstone of natural fertilizers. Create your own compost by collecting kitchen scraps, yard waste, and other organic materials. Compost is rich in nutrients, improves soil structure, and enhances microbial activity. Use it as a soil amendment or apply it as a top dressing around plants for slow-release nutrition.
2. Manure Magic: Animal manure is an excellent source of organic nutrients. However, it should be aged or composted before use to prevent burning plants. Chicken, cow, horse, and rabbit manure are commonly used. Apply well-aged manure to your garden beds or mix it into your compost pile to boost nutrient content.
3. Nutrient-Rich Bone Meal: Bone meal is derived from finely ground animal bones and is an excellent natural source of phosphorus. It helps promote root development and flowering in plants. Use bone meal sparingly, especially for phosphorus-loving plants like flowering bulbs, roses, and fruiting crops.
4. Mighty Fish Emulsion: Fish emulsion is a liquid fertilizer made from fish waste and is a rich source of nitrogen, phosphorus, and trace elements. Dilute it with water and

apply it to your plants. It promotes healthy leaf growth and is especially beneficial for vegetables, leafy greens, and annual flowers.
5. Epsom Salt Elixir: Epsom salt, or magnesium sulfate, is a natural fertilizer that provides magnesium and sulfur to plants. It promotes chlorophyll production, aids in nutrient absorption, and enhances overall plant health. Dissolve Epsom salt in water and apply it as a foliar spray or incorporate it into the soil around plants.
6. Seaweed Sensation: Seaweed or kelp extracts are fantastic natural fertilizers rich in trace minerals, growth hormones, and beneficial microorganisms. They boost plant vigor, stimulate root growth, and improve overall plant resilience. Apply as a foliar spray or use them as a soil drench for optimal results.
7. Vermicompost - Worm Power: Vermicompost, also known as worm castings, is the nutrient-rich byproduct of earthworms digesting organic matter. It is a superb natural fertilizer that enhances soil structure, promotes beneficial microbial activity, and enriches plant growth. Use it as a top dressing or mix it into potting soil for container gardening.
8. Green Tea - Liquid Energy: Brew a batch of green tea, let it cool, and use it as a liquid fertilizer. Green tea contains beneficial compounds that nourish plants and improve soil health. It can be applied directly to the soil or used as a foliar spray.
9. Banana Peel Power: Don't discard those banana peels! Rich in potassium and other essential nutrients, banana peels can be dried and ground into a powder or buried directly in the soil to provide a natural boost to potassium-

loving plants like tomatoes, peppers, and roses.
10. Harness the Power of Weeds: Some common weeds, such as nettle, comfrey, and dandelion, are rich in nutrients. Use them to make nutrient-rich teas or infusions by steeping them in water. After a few weeks, strain the liquid and use it to feed your plants.

Remember to follow proper application rates and frequency for natural fertilizers to avoid over-fertilization. With natural fertilizers, you'll not only nourish your plants but also promote a healthier soil ecosystem, reduce environmental impact, and create a more sustainable garden. Embrace the power of nature's bounty and watch your garden thrive!

#61 Use eggshells and coffee grounds: They add calcium and nitrogen to your soil.

The Eggshells and Coffee Grounds Hack: Boosting Soil Health and Plant Growth

Eggshells and coffee grounds are two kitchen waste items that can provide incredible benefits when used in your garden. They're readily available, cost-effective, and help create a more sustainable gardening practice. Let's explore the advantages of incorporating eggshells and coffee grounds into your gardening routine:

1. Eggshells for Calcium Boost: Eggshells are an excellent source of calcium, which is vital for plant growth and development. Crushed eggshells can be added directly to the soil or compost pile. Their calcium content helps prevent

blossom end rot in tomatoes and peppers and strengthens cell walls in various plants, promoting healthy growth.
2. Coffee Grounds for Organic Matter and Nutrients: Coffee grounds are a valuable source of organic matter that improves soil structure and enhances moisture retention. When added to the soil or compost, they gradually release nutrients like nitrogen, potassium, and phosphorus. Coffee grounds also attract earthworms, which further enhance soil health.
3. Supplement Soil with Eggshells: Crushed eggshells can be sprinkled around plants or worked into the soil to enrich it with calcium. This is particularly beneficial for calcium-loving plants like tomatoes, peppers, and squash. The eggshells slowly break down, releasing calcium into the soil over time.
4. Compost with Eggshells and Coffee Grounds: Incorporating eggshells and coffee grounds into your compost pile adds valuable nutrients and organic matter. The calcium from eggshells and the nitrogen from coffee grounds contribute to the overall nutrient balance in the compost. The resulting compost becomes a nutrient-rich soil amendment for your garden beds.
5. Pest Deterrent: Crushed eggshells can act as a natural deterrent for soft-bodied garden pests like slugs and snails. Create a barrier around vulnerable plants by sprinkling crushed eggshells to discourage these pests from reaching your plants.
6. Acidity Regulation: Coffee grounds have a slightly acidic pH, making them beneficial for plants that thrive in acidic soil, such as blueberries, azaleas, and rhododendrons. Incorporating coffee grounds into the soil can help maintain

the desired pH levels for these acid-loving plants.
7. Improving Soil Drainage and Aeration: Both eggshells and coffee grounds contribute to improving soil drainage and aeration. Eggshells create small air pockets as they break down, promoting better soil structure. Coffee grounds help loosen compacted soil, allowing better water infiltration and root development.
8. Sustainable Waste Management: Using eggshells and coffee grounds in your garden is an eco-friendly way to repurpose kitchen waste. Instead of discarding these items, you can recycle them into valuable resources for your plants, reducing landfill waste and embracing a more sustainable gardening approach.
9. Encouraging Earthworm Activity: Earthworms play a crucial role in soil health and nutrient cycling. Both eggshells and coffee grounds attract earthworms to your garden, promoting natural aeration, nutrient distribution, and the breakdown of organic matter.
10. Plant Nutrition and Growth: The nutrients released from eggshells and coffee grounds gradually nourish plants, supporting healthy growth, vibrant foliage, and abundant blooms. By incorporating these natural additives into your gardening routine, you provide essential elements that plants need for optimal development.

Remember to crush eggshells into small pieces for easier decomposition and consider balancing the use of coffee grounds with other organic materials. Embrace the advantages of using eggshells and coffee grounds in your garden, and witness the positive impact on soil health, plant growth

CHAPTER 8 FERTILIZERS

#62 Start a worm farm: Worm castings are an excellent soil amendment.

The Worm Farming Hack: Harnessing the Power of Vermiculture

Starting a worm farm, also known as vermiculture, is an excellent way to recycle kitchen scraps, reduce waste, and create nutrient-rich vermicompost for your garden. Worms are nature's little helpers, breaking down organic matter and producing nutrient-rich castings. Here's how to get started with your own worm farm:

1. Select the Right Worms: Choose red wigglers (Eisenia fetida) or tiger worms (Eisenia andreii) for your worm farm. These worms are efficient decomposers and thrive in organic waste-rich environments.
2. Choose a Suitable Container: Select a container for your worm farm, such as a plastic bin, wooden box, or specialized worm composting system. Ensure the container has a lid to create a dark and moist environment for the worms.
3. Create a Bedding Layer: Prepare a bedding layer for your worms using a mix of shredded newspaper, cardboard, and coconut coir. Dampen the bedding material with water until it reaches the consistency of a wrung-out sponge.
4. Introduce the Worms: Gently place the worms on top of the bedding layer. Start with a small population, around 500 to 1,000 worms, and gradually increase their numbers as the worm farm matures.
5. Feed Your Worms: Provide a balanced diet for your worms by feeding them a variety of kitchen scraps. They enjoy fruit and vegetable scraps, coffee grounds, tea bags,

crushed eggshells, and small amounts of non-greasy food leftovers. Avoid feeding them meat, dairy, oily products, or heavily processed foods.

6. Maintain Moisture and Temperature: Worms prefer a moist environment, so periodically check the moisture levels in the bedding. Spray water if it feels too dry or add dry bedding if it's too wet. Keep the worm farm in a cool, shaded area to prevent overheating.
7. Cover and Ventilate: Place a lid on the worm farm to create darkness and discourage pests. However, ensure proper ventilation by drilling small holes in the lid or sides of the container to allow airflow.
8. Harvest the Vermicompost: After several months, the worms will transform the organic waste into vermicompost. Harvest the vermicompost by gently separating it from the worms. You can use the "migration method" by creating a new bedding area and placing fresh food there. The worms will migrate to the new area, allowing you to harvest the vermicompost from the previous section.
9. Use Vermicompost in the Garden: Incorporate the vermicompost into your garden soil as a nutrient-rich amendment. Mix it into potting soil for container gardening or apply it as a top dressing around plants. Your plants will benefit from the enhanced soil fertility and improved nutrient availability.
10. Continue Feeding and Maintaining: As your worm farm matures, continue feeding your worms regularly and maintaining optimal conditions. Monitor the moisture levels, adjust the bedding as needed, and provide a balanced diet to ensure the health and productivity of your worm farm.

CHAPTER 8 FERTILIZERS

Starting a worm farm allows you to recycle kitchen waste, produce nutrient-rich vermicompost, and cultivate a more sustainable gardening practice. With the help of these amazing little creatures, you'll witness the transformation of organic waste into black gold and the remarkable impact it has on your garden's health and productivity. Enjoy the wonders of vermiculture and embrace the power of worms in your gardening journey!

#63 Use aspirin to boost plant immune systems: Dissolve an aspirin in water and water your plants with it to boost their disease resistance.

The Aspirin Hack: Enhancing Plant Immune Systems Naturally
Believe it or not, aspirin, a common household medication, can have a positive impact on your plants' immune systems. Aspirin contains a compound called salicylic acid, which can help plants defend against diseases, pests, and environmental stressors. Here's how to use aspirin to boost your plants' immune systems:

1. Prepare the Aspirin Solution: Dissolve one regular-strength, uncoated aspirin tablet (325 mg) in one gallon (3.8 liters) of water. Alternatively, you can crush the aspirin tablet into a fine powder before mixing it with the water. Stir the solution until the aspirin is completely dissolved.
2. Choose the Right Timing: Apply the aspirin solution to your plants during periods of stress or before potential disease outbreaks. For example, you can apply it after

extreme weather conditions, transplanting, or when you notice early signs of disease.
3. Test on a Small Area: Before treating all your plants, it's best to conduct a patch test on a small, inconspicuous area of a few plants to ensure they don't have any adverse reactions. Monitor the test area for a couple of days to observe any negative effects.
4. Apply as a Foliar Spray: Use a spray bottle or garden sprayer to apply the aspirin solution as a foliar spray. Make sure to thoroughly cover the leaves, stems, and surrounding soil. A fine mist or spray is sufficient to coat the plant surfaces.
5. Avoid Sunlight Exposure: Apply the aspirin solution during the early morning or late afternoon to minimize sun exposure. This helps prevent potential leaf burn caused by the interaction between aspirin and sunlight.
6. Repeat at Intervals: For optimal results, repeat the aspirin application every two to three weeks or as needed, especially during periods of high disease pressure or stress. However, avoid excessive or prolonged use, as it can have negative effects on plant growth.
7. Observe and Monitor: Keep a close eye on your plants after applying the aspirin solution. Look for any signs of improvement in disease resistance or overall plant health. Note any adverse effects, such as leaf discoloration or wilting, and discontinue use if these issues persist.
8. Combine with Good Cultural Practices: Remember that aspirin is not a cure-all solution. To maximize the benefits, ensure you follow good cultural practices, such as providing proper watering, adequate sunlight, and well-draining soil. Additionally, maintain good garden hygiene

by removing diseased plant material and practicing crop rotation.
9. Use with Caution: It's important to note that not all plants may respond positively to aspirin. Some plant species are more sensitive than others, so always test on a small area first and observe the plant's reaction before treating the entire garden.
10. Focus on Prevention: While aspirin can help boost a plant's immune system, it's crucial to prioritize prevention in your gardening practices. Provide plants with optimal growing conditions, practice good sanitation, and select disease-resistant varieties to minimize the need for interventions.

By using aspirin to boost your plants' immune systems, you can potentially enhance their ability to fight diseases, resist pests, and overcome environmental stressors. Remember, however, that aspirin is not a substitute for good gardening practices. It should be used in conjunction with proper care and maintenance to create a thriving and resilient garden.

#64 Use Epsom salt for better blooms: It provides magnesium, which helps plant roots take up vital nutrients.

The Epsom Salt Hack: Promoting Plant Health and Vigor
Epsom salt, also known as magnesium sulfate, is a versatile and cost-effective natural substance that can benefit your garden in several ways. It provides essential nutrients and minerals, enhances plant growth, improves nutrient absorption, and helps with pest control. Here's how to make the most of

Epsom salt in your garden:

1. Soil Preparation: Prior to planting, incorporate Epsom salt into your garden soil to improve soil structure and nutrient availability. Sprinkle a handful of Epsom salt per square foot (30 cm) evenly over the soil surface, then mix it in thoroughly.
2. Seed Starting Boost: Give your seeds a head start by soaking them in an Epsom salt solution before planting. Dissolve one tablespoon of Epsom salt in one gallon (3.8 liters) of water, and soak the seeds for a few hours or overnight. This can enhance germination rates and provide a nutritional boost to seedlings.
3. Foliar Spray for Greenery: Create a foliar spray using Epsom salt to promote lush green foliage. Dissolve two tablespoons of Epsom salt in one gallon (3.8 liters) of water. Spray the solution directly on the leaves of plants such as tomatoes, peppers, and leafy greens. This helps prevent magnesium deficiency and enhances chlorophyll production.
4. Enhanced Flowering and Fruit Set: To encourage abundant blooms and fruiting, dissolve two tablespoons of Epsom salt in one gallon (3.8 liters) of water. Apply this solution to flowering plants, fruit trees, or vegetable crops during the blooming period. The magnesium in the Epsom salt can support healthy flower and fruit development.
5. Revitalize Potted Plants: Over time, potted plants can suffer from nutrient deficiencies due to leaching and limited access to natural minerals. Sprinkle a teaspoon of Epsom salt on the soil surface around the base of your potted plants. Water thoroughly to allow the Epsom salt

to dissolve and provide a nutrient boost.
6. Tomato and Pepper Care: Epsom salt is particularly beneficial for tomato and pepper plants. Incorporate one tablespoon of Epsom salt into the planting hole or sprinkle it around the base of established plants. This supports overall plant health, strengthens cell walls, and helps prevent blossom end rot.
7. Pest Deterrent: Epsom salt can also help deter pests in the garden. Sprinkle a line of Epsom salt around susceptible plants to repel slugs and snails. The abrasive texture deters them from crossing the barrier, protecting your plants naturally.
8. Roses and Blooming Shrubs: Roses and blooming shrubs can benefit from Epsom salt to promote healthier growth and more vibrant blooms. Dissolve one tablespoon of Epsom salt in one gallon (3.8 liters) of water, and apply it around the base of the plants every four to six weeks during the growing season.
9. Reviving Yellowing Plants: If your plants are showing signs of yellowing leaves, it could indicate a magnesium deficiency. Dissolve two tablespoons of Epsom salt in one gallon (3.8 liters) of water and apply it as a soil drench to help correct the deficiency and restore plant health.
10. Proper Usage and Caution: While Epsom salt can be beneficial, it's essential to use it in moderation. Avoid over-application, as excessive amounts can harm plants or disrupt soil pH. It's always best to conduct a soil test to determine if your plants specifically require additional magnesium or sulfur.

By using Epsom salt as a natural supplement in your gardening routine, you can improve soil fertility, support plant growth, and address nutrient deficiencies. Enjoy the benefits of this versatile substance and watch your garden thrive with healthier, more vibrant plants.

#65 Use banana peels as a natural fertilizer: They decompose quickly and provide potassium.

The Banana Peel Fertilizer Hack: Harnessing Nutrient Power for Your Garden

Don't toss those banana peels into the compost bin just yet! Banana peels are packed with valuable nutrients that can benefit your plants and help reduce waste. With this simple gardening hack, you can turn banana peels into a natural fertilizer for your garden. Here's how to do it:

1. Collect and Prepare the Banana Peels: Save banana peels from your kitchen and let them dry out for a few days. Once dry, cut them into smaller pieces to speed up decomposition and make it easier for your plants to absorb the nutrients.
2. Direct Application: One way to use banana peels is to bury them directly in the soil around your plants. Dig a small hole near the base of the plant and place a few pieces of the banana peel into the hole. Cover them with soil and water gently. As the banana peels break down, they release nutrients into the soil, enriching it and benefiting your plants.
3. Composting with Banana Peels: Another option is to add banana peels to your compost pile. Chop the peels into

smaller pieces and mix them in with other compostable materials, such as kitchen scraps, yard waste, and dry leaves. The peels will break down over time, contributing valuable nutrients to the compost. Incorporate the finished compost into your garden beds to provide a nutrient-rich boost to your plants.
4. Banana Peel Tea: Create a nutrient-rich liquid fertilizer by making banana peel tea. Place a few banana peels in a container, cover them with water, and let them soak for several days or up to a week. Stir the mixture occasionally. The water will gradually absorb the nutrients from the peels. Strain the liquid and dilute it with water at a ratio of 1:2 or 1:3 (banana peel tea to water). Use this diluted solution to water your plants every few weeks for an extra nutritional boost.
5. Targeted Applications: Some plants, like roses, tomatoes, and peppers, particularly benefit from the nutrients in banana peels. Consider applying banana peels around these specific plants to support their growth and flowering. The potassium and phosphorus in banana peels can promote healthy blooms and fruit set.
6. Avoid Overuse: While banana peels are beneficial, it's important to use them in moderation. Overusing banana peels as fertilizer can result in an imbalance of nutrients or excessive potassium levels, which may affect plant growth. Aim for a balanced approach by combining banana peels with other organic fertilizers and following recommended application rates.
7. Additional Uses: Aside from being a natural fertilizer, banana peels can serve other purposes in the garden. Use them to deter pests like aphids or attract beneficial insects

like butterflies and bees. You can also place small pieces of banana peel directly on the soil surface to suppress weed growth around your plants.

By utilizing banana peels as a natural fertilizer, you can reduce waste, enhance soil fertility, and nourish your plants with valuable nutrients. Embrace this sustainable gardening hack and watch your garden thrive with the power of nutrient-rich banana peels.

10

Chapter 9 Garden Care and Maintenance

#66 Regular pruning: This helps to improve the health and productivity of your plants.

The Regular Pruning Hack: Unlocking the Benefits for Your Plants

Pruning is a vital gardening practice that offers numerous benefits for the health, appearance, and productivity of your plants. By regularly pruning your plants, you can unlock their full potential and create a more vibrant and well-maintained garden. Here's why regular pruning is advantageous:

1. Encourages Healthy Growth: Pruning helps stimulate healthy growth in plants. By selectively removing dead, damaged, or diseased branches, you allow the plant to direct its energy towards new growth and overall vitality. Pruning also promotes the development of strong and sturdy branches, enhancing the plant's structural integrity.
2. Enhances Plant Appearance: Regular pruning improves the overall appearance and aesthetics of your plants. By removing overgrown or unruly branches, you can maintain a neat and well-groomed appearance. Pruning can also encourage a more compact and bushy growth habit, resulting in a more visually appealing and balanced plant shape.
3. Increases Air Circulation: Proper pruning creates better airflow within the plant canopy, reducing the risk of fungal diseases. Improved air circulation helps to dry foliage quickly after rain or irrigation, minimizing the chance of mold or mildew development. It also prevents the buildup of excessive moisture that can attract pests or lead to fungal infections.
4. Promotes Flowering and Fruit Production: Pruning plays a crucial role in promoting abundant flowering and fruit production. By selectively removing old or spent flower heads, you encourage the plant to redirect its energy

towards producing new blooms. Proper pruning also improves light penetration, enabling more even bud formation and maximizing fruiting potential.
5. Controls Plant Size and Shape: Pruning allows you to control the size and shape of your plants. By selectively trimming back branches, you can prevent overcrowding, maintain a manageable size, and prevent plants from outgrowing their allotted space. This is particularly useful for hedges, shrubs, and trees that require regular maintenance to stay in their desired form.
6. Revitalizes Overgrown Plants: Over time, some plants may become leggy or overgrown. Pruning provides an opportunity to rejuvenate these plants. By removing a portion of the old growth, you can stimulate new growth from the base, resulting in a more compact and rejuvenated plant.
7. Improves Sunlight Penetration: Proper pruning opens up the plant canopy, allowing better sunlight penetration to reach lower leaves and branches. This is especially important for plants that require ample sunlight for optimal growth and flowering. Increased sunlight exposure promotes photosynthesis, leading to healthier and more vigorous plants.
8. Maintains Plant Health: Regular pruning helps identify and address potential pest or disease issues early on. By removing affected branches or leaves promptly, you can prevent the spread of pests or diseases to other parts of the plant or nearby plants. Pruning also allows for better inspection of the plant, enabling you to spot any signs of stress or damage that require attention.
9. Shape and Structure for Training: Pruning is essential for training certain plants into desired shapes or forms.

It's particularly relevant for topiaries, espaliers, or plants grown against trellises or supports. By carefully pruning and shaping the plant, you can create intricate designs or control its growth to fit specific spaces or structures.
10. Promotes Long-Term Plant Health: Overall, regular pruning contributes to the long-term health and longevity of your plants. It helps maintain plant vigor, reduces the risk of disease, improves flowering and fruiting, and keeps plants looking their best. With proper pruning, you'll enjoy a healthier, more visually appealing garden for years to come.

Remember to use clean, sharp tools and follow proper pruning techniques for each plant species. Timing and approach may vary, so consult plant-specific guides or seek advice from local gardening resources. Embrace the advantages of regular pruning and watch your plants thrive with enhanced growth, beauty, and productivity.

#67 Use garden fabric: This can protect your plants from frost in early spring or late fall.

The Garden Fabric Hack: Protecting and Enhancing Your Plants Naturally

Garden fabric, also known as row cover or plant cover, is a versatile tool that can greatly benefit your garden. This lightweight and breathable material provides a protective barrier for your plants, shielding them from pests, extreme weather, and other environmental challenges. Here's how to make the most of garden fabric in your gardening endeavors:

1. Pest Protection: Garden fabric acts as a physical barrier,

preventing pests like insects, birds, and rabbits from accessing your plants. Cover susceptible crops with garden fabric, securing the edges to create a sealed environment. This helps deter pests from damaging your plants and reduces the need for chemical interventions.
2. Frost and Cold Protection: Garden fabric can safeguard your plants from frost and cold temperatures. When frost is expected, cover vulnerable plants with the fabric, anchoring it securely to the ground. The fabric acts as insulation, trapping heat from the soil and creating a microclimate around the plants. This protects them from freezing temperatures and minimizes frost damage.
3. Wind and Sun Protection: Garden fabric offers protection against harsh winds and intense sunlight. Use it to create windbreaks for delicate plants or to shield sun-sensitive crops during the hottest hours of the day. The fabric reduces wind stress, prevents excessive drying, and helps maintain optimal growing conditions.
4. Season Extension: Garden fabric can extend the growing season by providing an extra layer of insulation. By covering plants early in spring or late in autumn, you can create a warmer environment that promotes earlier growth or protects against early frosts. This allows you to enjoy fresh produce for longer periods and experiment with a wider variety of crops.
5. Moisture Retention: Garden fabric helps retain moisture in the soil by reducing evaporation. When laid over the soil surface, it acts as a barrier, preventing water from escaping too quickly. This is especially beneficial in hot and arid climates or during dry spells, where water conservation is crucial for plant health.

6. Weed Control: Garden fabric can help suppress weed growth and minimize competition for nutrients and water. When properly installed, it creates a barrier that inhibits weed germination and growth. Before laying the fabric, remove existing weeds and cover the soil with mulch for added effectiveness.
7. Light and Air Circulation: Garden fabric allows light and air to penetrate while still providing protection. This ensures that your plants receive the necessary light for photosynthesis and ample airflow to prevent the development of fungal diseases. Opt for lightweight fabric or choose specific types designed for optimal light transmission.
8. Easy Installation and Customization: Garden fabric is easy to install and customize to fit your garden needs. It comes in rolls or sheets that can be cut to the desired size. Use stakes, hoops, or clips to hold the fabric in place and create a secure enclosure for your plants. For taller plants, choose fabric with extra height or construct a frame to accommodate their growth.
9. Reusable and Environmentally Friendly: Garden fabric is reusable, making it an eco-friendly choice for your garden. After each season, carefully remove the fabric, clean it if necessary, and store it for future use. With proper care, garden fabric can last for several growing seasons, reducing waste and saving money.
10. Monitor and Adjust: While garden fabric offers protection, it's important to monitor your plants regularly. Check for signs of pests, disease, or moisture levels. Adjust the fabric as needed to provide adequate ventilation, prevent overheating, or accommodate plant growth.

CHAPTER 9 GARDEN CARE AND MAINTENANCE

By incorporating garden fabric into your gardening routine, you can provide a protective shield for your plants, extend the growing season, conserve moisture, and create optimal growing conditions.

#68 Be patient: Gardening is a slow process. Don't expect instant results.

The Patience Hack: Cultivating Growth and Enjoyment through Time

Patience is a virtue in gardening, and it plays a vital role in your gardening journey. While we often crave instant results, understanding the value of patience can lead to more fulfilling and successful gardening experiences. Here's why patience is essential in gardening:

1. Natural Growth Processes: Just as it takes time for a seed to sprout and grow into a mature plant, patience is required to witness the natural growth processes of your garden. Embracing this journey allows you to appreciate every stage of development, from seed to harvest, and enjoy the beauty of nature unfolding before your eyes.
2. Establishing Healthy Roots: Patience is crucial during the early stages of plant growth when roots are developing. By allowing plants sufficient time to establish a strong root system, you promote their long-term health and resilience. Strong roots provide better access to nutrients and water, leading to healthier and more productive plants in the future.
3. Adapting to Seasonal Changes: Gardening is closely tied to the seasons, and each season brings its own set of challenges and rewards. Patience is key when navigating

the ebb and flow of the seasons. Understanding that growth rates, flowering times, and harvests are influenced by seasonal variations allows you to adjust expectations and embrace the natural rhythm of the garden.

4. Overcoming Setbacks and Learning: Gardening often involves setbacks such as pest infestations, diseases, or unfavorable weather conditions. Patience helps you persevere through these challenges and learn from them. By remaining patient, you can assess the situation, make necessary adjustments, and implement preventative measures to prevent future setbacks.

5. Enjoying the Journey: Gardening is not just about the end result; it's about the joy and fulfillment that comes from the process itself. Patience allows you to savor every moment spent in the garden, observing the intricate details of each plant, and connecting with nature. It offers an opportunity to slow down, unwind, and appreciate the therapeutic aspects of gardening.

6. Gardening as a Learning Experience: Patience in gardening goes hand in hand with continuous learning. Gardening teaches us the value of patience as we experiment with different techniques, learn from failures, and refine our skills. Each season presents an opportunity to grow as a gardener and deepen our understanding of the natural world.

7. Building Resilience and Perseverance: Patience in gardening cultivates resilience and perseverance. It teaches us that not every plant will thrive, not every seed will sprout, and not every harvest will be bountiful. Yet, by remaining patient and persistent, we learn to adapt, problem-solve, and ultimately become better gardeners.

CHAPTER 9 GARDEN CARE AND MAINTENANCE

8. Appreciating the Slow Beauty: Patience enables us to appreciate the beauty of slow and gradual transformations in the garden. From the delicate unfolding of a flower bud to the gradual color change of autumn leaves, patience allows us to witness and celebrate nature's artistic expressions.
9. Rewarding Harvests: Patience in gardening is often rewarded with plentiful harvests. Many fruits, vegetables, and herbs require time to ripen and reach their peak flavor. By patiently waiting for the right moment to harvest, you can enjoy the fullness of nature's bounty and savor the rewards of your labor.
10. Gardening as a Mindful Practice: Patience in gardening offers an opportunity to practice mindfulness. By being fully present in the garden, observing, and tending to each plant's needs, you cultivate a sense of peace and contentment. Gardening becomes a meditative practice that allows you to reconnect with nature and find solace in the beauty of the natural world.

Remember, gardening is a journey that requires time, attention, and patience. By embracing the art of waiting, you not only nurture your plants but also cultivate inner growth, resilience, and a deep appreciation for the wonders of the natural world. Enjoy the process, be patient, and allow your garden to unfold its magic in due time.

#69 Clean up in the fall: Remove dead plants and leaves to prevent diseases and pests from overwintering.

The Fall Cleanup Hack: Setting the Stage for a Successful Garden

As the growing season comes to a close, undertaking a thorough fall cleanup in your garden is essential for its long-term health and success. While it may seem like a daunting task, this process sets the stage for a fresh start in the following year. Here's why fall cleanup is important and how you can make the most of it:

1. Pest and Disease Prevention: Cleaning up fallen leaves, plant debris, and spent vegetation helps prevent the buildup of pests and diseases. Many pests and diseases overwinter in garden debris, providing a breeding ground for future infestations. By removing and properly disposing of this debris, you break the lifecycle and reduce the risk of pests and diseases affecting your garden next year.
2. Weed Control: Fall cleanup is an opportunity to tackle weeds and prevent them from reseeding or spreading throughout your garden. Remove any weeds that have emerged and dispose of them properly to minimize the chances of their return. By addressing weeds in the fall, you reduce competition for nutrients and space, giving your desirable plants a better start in the spring.
3. Encourages Soil Health: Cleaning up in the fall allows you to assess the condition of your soil and take steps to improve its health. Clearing away plant debris and fallen leaves prevents them from decomposing on the soil surface, which can lead to nutrient imbalances or encourage the growth of harmful fungi. This promotes better soil drainage, reduces the risk of soil-borne diseases, and prepares the ground for future amendments or cover cropping.
4. Prevents Overwintering Pests: Many insects and pests

overwinter in garden debris, such as fallen leaves or hollow plant stems. By removing these potential shelters, you disrupt their hibernation sites and minimize the population of pests that could emerge in the following year. This natural pest control method helps maintain a healthier garden ecosystem.

5. Assessment and Planning: Fall cleanup provides an opportunity to assess the overall condition of your garden. Take note of any areas that may need improvements, such as soil amendments, drainage adjustments, or structural repairs. As you tidy up, make observations about plant performance and identify any changes or adjustments you may want to make for the next growing season. This assessment helps you plan and prepare for future gardening endeavors.

6. Enhances Aesthetics: A well-maintained garden offers visual appeal even during the dormant winter months. Fall cleanup tidies up the garden, removing dead plants and debris that can make your garden appear messy or unkempt. By creating a clean and organized space, you set the stage for a beautiful garden come springtime.

7. Prevents Seed Dispersal: Clearing out spent plants and seed heads in the fall prevents the dispersal of seeds that can become invasive or undesirable in your garden. By removing these potential weed sources, you reduce the likelihood of unwanted plants taking over your garden beds.

8. Preparation for Winter Protection: Fall cleanup also involves preparing your garden for winter protection. Remove any plant supports, trellises, or stakes that are no longer needed. Properly clean and store these items to

ensure their longevity. Additionally, consider applying a layer of mulch to insulate the soil and protect the root systems of perennials during the winter months.
9. Time and Energy Savings: Cleaning up in the fall saves time and energy in the long run. By addressing garden maintenance tasks before winter arrives, you can start the next gardening season with a clean slate. This reduces the workload in the spring and allows you to focus on planting and other gardening activities rather than dealing with last year's debris.
10. Promotes a Fresh Start: Fall cleanup sets the stage for a fresh start in the next gardening season. It clears the way for new growth, healthier plants, and a more organized and efficient garden space. Embrace the opportunity to tidy up, reflect on your gardening experiences, and anticipate the potential that the coming year holds.

Remember to compost or dispose of plant debris properly, ensuring that any diseased or pest-infested material is removed from the garden completely. By incorporating a thorough fall cleanup routine, you contribute to the long-term success and vitality of your garden.

11

Chapter 10 Pests and Insects

#70 Protect from pests: Use organic pesticides and consider physical barriers for pests.

The Organic Pest Control Hack: Nurturing a Healthy Garden Naturally

Maintaining a pest-free garden is crucial for the health and productivity of your plants. Instead of relying on chemical pesticides, you can adopt organic pest control methods that are safe, environmentally friendly, and effective. By utilizing organic pesticides and physical barriers, you can protect your plants from pests while maintaining a healthy and thriving garden. Here's how to make the most of these methods:

1. Identify and Monitor Pests: Regularly inspect your garden for signs of pest activity, such as chewed leaves, holes, or insect presence. Identify the specific pests causing damage to determine the appropriate organic control measures.
2. Encourage Beneficial Insects: Promote a natural balance

in your garden by attracting beneficial insects that prey on pests. Plant flowers such as marigolds, lavender, and dill to attract ladybugs, lacewings, and parasitic wasps. These beneficial insects help control common garden pests like aphids, mites, and caterpillars.
3. Homemade Organic Pesticides: Create your own organic pesticides using common kitchen ingredients. For example, a solution of diluted dish soap and water can be sprayed on aphids or soft-bodied pests. Neem oil is effective against a wide range of pests, including beetles, caterpillars, and mites. Garlic or chili pepper sprays can deter chewing insects. Remember to follow application instructions and avoid spraying during peak sunlight hours to prevent leaf damage.
4. Beneficial Nematodes: Utilize beneficial nematodes, microscopic worms that attack soil-dwelling pests like grubs and larvae. These natural predators are available as a powder or liquid that can be applied to the soil according to the package instructions. Beneficial nematodes are safe for plants, humans, and pets.
5. Physical Barriers: Install physical barriers to protect your plants from pests. Use row covers or garden fabric to create a protective shield that prevents insects from reaching your plants. This method is particularly effective against flying pests like moths and butterflies. Secure the covers firmly to the ground to prevent pests from crawling underneath.
6. Companion Planting: Take advantage of companion planting to naturally deter pests. Some plants, such as marigolds, basil, and mint, have natural insect-repellent properties. Interplant these pest-repellent

plants among your susceptible crops to create a deterrent effect. Additionally, some plant combinations attract beneficial insects, creating a natural defense against pests.
7. Crop Rotation: Practice crop rotation to minimize pest problems. Pests often have specific host plants they target, and by rotating your crops each season, you disrupt their lifecycle and reduce the likelihood of pest buildup in the soil.
8. Handpicking: Sometimes, physically removing pests by hand is the most effective method. Regularly inspect your plants and manually remove pests like caterpillars, snails, or beetles. Drop them into a bucket of soapy water or relocate them away from your garden.
9. Beer Traps and Slug Deterrents: For slug control, bury shallow containers filled with beer near slug-prone areas. Slugs are attracted to the beer and will crawl into the container, where they will drown. You can also use diatomaceous earth, crushed eggshells, or copper tape to create physical barriers that deter slugs and snails.
10. Good Garden Hygiene: Practicing good garden hygiene is essential for pest control. Remove plant debris, fallen fruits, and weeds regularly, as they can harbor pests or provide hiding spots. This reduces pest habitats and minimizes the risk of infestations.

Remember that organic pest control methods require patience and consistent application. Observe your plants regularly, adapt your pest control strategies as needed, and maintain a balanced ecosystem in your garden. By harnessing the power of organic pesticides and physical barriers, you can nurture a healthy garden naturally while minimizing harm to beneficial insects and the environment.

#71 Encourage beneficial insects: Plants like daisies and sunflowers attract ladybugs and other beneficial insects that eat pests.

The Beneficial Insect Hack: Cultivating a Haven for Garden Allies

Beneficial insects play a vital role in maintaining a healthy garden ecosystem by preying on harmful pests, pollinating flowers, and contributing to overall biodiversity. By creating a welcoming environment for these helpful allies, you can naturally reduce pest populations and promote a thriving garden. Here's how to encourage beneficial insects:

1. Plant a Diversity of Flowers: Choose a variety of flowering plants that provide nectar and pollen throughout the growing season. Opt for native plant species, as they are well-adapted to your local ecosystem and attract a wide range of beneficial insects. Include flowers such as lavender, sunflowers, marigolds, zinnias, and daisies to entice pollinators and beneficial insects to visit your garden.
2. Create a Water Source: Beneficial insects need a water source to thrive. Provide shallow dishes or saucers filled with fresh water to serve as drinking spots for bees, butterflies, and other beneficial insects. Add a few small stones or pebbles to the water to create perches for them to rest on while drinking.
3. Install Insect Hotels: Build or purchase insect hotels to provide nesting sites for beneficial insects. These hotels

CHAPTER 10 PESTS AND INSECTS

consist of small cavities or tubes where insects like solitary bees, ladybugs, and lacewings can lay their eggs. Place the insect hotels in a sunny, sheltered location in your garden, preferably near flowering plants and a water source.

4. Use Minimal Pesticides: Minimize the use of chemical pesticides, as they can harm beneficial insects along with harmful pests. Instead, opt for organic pest control methods that target specific pests while preserving beneficial insects. By reducing pesticide use, you create a safer environment for beneficial insects to thrive.
5. Avoid Excessive Garden Cleanup: Leave some areas of your garden undisturbed, allowing natural debris and fallen leaves to accumulate. Beneficial insects often overwinter in these areas, seeking shelter and protection. Providing these hiding spots helps support their populations and encourages their return year after year.
6. Attract Predatory Insects: Certain flowering plants, such as yarrow, dill, and fennel, attract predatory insects like ladybugs, lacewings, and hoverflies. These insects feed on pests like aphids, mites, and caterpillars. By including these plants in your garden, you create a natural buffet that entices beneficial predators to stay and help control pest populations.
7. Avoid Excessive Mulching: While mulching offers benefits like weed suppression and moisture retention, it can also discourage ground-dwelling beneficial insects. Avoid heavy mulching in certain areas to provide exposed soil patches where ground beetles, spiders, and predatory wasps can hunt for pests.
8. Plant Beneficial Insect Attractors: Some plants specifically attract beneficial insects due to their nectar, pollen, or

aromatic compounds. Examples include daisies, alyssum, cosmos, and milkweed. By incorporating these attractor plants into your garden, you'll draw in a diverse array of beneficial insects.
9. Encourage Hoverflies and Parasitic Wasps: Hoverflies and parasitic wasps are excellent pest predators. To attract hoverflies, plant flowers with flat or shallow blooms, such as dill, fennel, and yarrow. Parasitic wasps, on the other hand, seek out nectar-producing plants like parsley, sweet alyssum, and tansy.
10. Be Mindful of Timing: Ensure that you have a continuous supply of flowering plants throughout the growing season. By staggering the blooming periods, you provide a consistent food source for beneficial insects throughout their active periods.

Remember, creating a garden haven for beneficial insects takes time. Be patient, observe the interactions in your garden, and make adjustments as needed. With their help, you'll maintain a balanced ecosystem and enjoy a healthier, pest-resistant garden.

#72 Solarize your soil: Use the sun's heat in the summer to kill off disease organisms and pests in your soil.
The Soil Solarization Hack: Harnessing the Sun's Power for Soil Health
Soil solarization is an effective, chemical-free method to naturally eliminate disease organisms, pests, and weed seeds from your garden soil. By utilizing the power of the sun's heat, you can create a hostile environment that stifles harmful organisms and promotes healthier soil. Here's how to make

CHAPTER 10 PESTS AND INSECTS

the most of soil solarization:

1. Choose the Right Time: Plan to solarize your soil during the hottest and sunniest period of the year, typically in the peak of summer. This ensures maximum heat intensity, which is crucial for the success of the solarization process.
2. Prepare the Soil: Before solarizing, clear the area of any weeds, rocks, or debris. Rake the soil to create a smooth surface, ensuring there are no clumps or large air pockets that could hinder the process. It's important to work with moist soil, so water the area thoroughly a day or two before starting the solarization process.
3. Cover the Soil: Lay a clear plastic sheet over the prepared soil, ensuring it completely covers the area. Use a sturdy, UV-stabilized plastic sheet that is at least 2 to 4 mils thick for optimal heat retention. Secure the edges of the plastic sheet with rocks, soil, or weights to hold it in place and create a sealed environment.
4. Maximize Heat Absorption: Smooth out any wrinkles or air pockets in the plastic sheet to maximize heat absorption. The plastic sheet acts like a greenhouse, trapping the sun's heat and raising the temperature in the soil beneath.
5. Leave the Plastic in Place: Allow the plastic sheet to remain in place for several weeks, ideally around four to six weeks, to ensure sufficient heat penetration. During this time, the soil temperature increases, reaching levels that are lethal to many disease organisms, pests, and weed seeds.
6. Monitor the Soil Temperature: Use a soil thermometer to monitor the temperature under the plastic sheet regularly. The desired temperature range for effective solarization is between 110°F and 125°F (43°C and 52°C). Adjust the

plastic sheet as needed to maintain optimal heat levels. Avoid exceeding temperatures above 130°F (54°C), as it may harm beneficial organisms in the soil.
7. Ensure Proper Contact: For better heat transfer, ensure the plastic sheet is in direct contact with the soil surface. This prevents cool air pockets from forming and promotes uniform heat distribution throughout the soil profile.
8. Extend the Solarization Period: In cooler climates or if you're dealing with particularly resilient pests or disease organisms, you can extend the solarization period to eight weeks or longer. This ensures thorough elimination of the targeted organisms.
9. Watering During Solarization: While the soil is covered, avoid watering or irrigating the area. The goal is to create a dry and hot environment that is inhospitable to pests and pathogens. However, if the soil becomes excessively dry or the plastic sheet loses contact with the soil, you can lightly water the area before resealing it to maintain adequate moisture.
10. Uncover and Plant: After the solarization period is complete, remove the plastic sheet and allow the soil to cool for a few days. At this point, the soil is free of many harmful organisms and weed seeds. You can now proceed to plant your desired crops, taking advantage of the rejuvenated, pest-free soil.

Soil solarization is a natural and effective method to cleanse your soil of pests, disease organisms, and weed seeds. Harness the power of the sun's heat, and watch your garden flourish with healthier plants and reduced pest problems.

CHAPTER 10 PESTS AND INSECTS

#73 Respect wildlife: Many animals, like birds and certain insects, can be beneficial for your garden.

The Wildlife-Friendly Garden Hack: Embracing Nature's Helpers

Creating a wildlife-friendly garden not only enhances the beauty of your outdoor space but also fosters a healthy ecosystem that supports a diverse array of beneficial wildlife. By respecting and attracting wildlife, you can harness their natural abilities to assist in pest control, pollination, and overall garden health. Here's how to make the most of wildlife in your garden:

1. Provide Shelter and Habitat: Designate areas of your garden to provide shelter and habitat for wildlife. Create brush piles, rock piles, or install birdhouses, bat boxes, or insect hotels. These structures offer nesting opportunities for birds, bats, insects, and other beneficial creatures, allowing them to establish a presence in your garden.
2. Encourage Native Plants: Incorporate a variety of native plants into your garden landscape. Native plants provide essential food sources, shelter, and nesting sites for local wildlife. They are well-adapted to the local ecosystem and attract a diverse range of beneficial insects, birds, and other wildlife that help maintain a healthy garden ecosystem.
3. Water Sources: Provide a water source, such as a birdbath, shallow dish, or small pond, for wildlife to drink and bathe. Ensure the water source is regularly refreshed to prevent stagnation and mosquito breeding. Wildlife, particularly birds and beneficial insects, will appreciate a reliable water supply, especially during hot and dry periods.
4. Avoid Chemical Pesticides: Minimize or eliminate the

use of chemical pesticides, as they can harm beneficial wildlife along with pests. Instead, focus on organic pest control methods and natural predators to manage pest populations. Beneficial insects, birds, toads, and other creatures often help keep pest populations in check if given the opportunity.

5. Create Pollinator-Friendly Areas: Incorporate plants that attract pollinators, such as bees, butterflies, and hummingbirds, into your garden. Choose a diverse range of flowering plants with different shapes, colors, and bloom times to provide nectar and pollen throughout the growing season. Pollinators play a crucial role in pollinating your plants, ensuring fruit set and seed production.

6. Provide Food Sources: Offer supplemental food sources for wildlife, especially during periods when natural food may be scarce. Install bird feeders and provide bird-friendly foods like seeds, suet, or fruit. Plant berry-producing shrubs or trees to attract birds and small mammals. Additionally, consider leaving some fruits or seeds from your garden crops for wildlife to enjoy.

7. Beneficial Insects: Encourage beneficial insects by creating diverse plantings and reducing pesticide use. Ladybugs, lacewings, predatory wasps, and hoverflies are just a few examples of beneficial insects that help control pest populations naturally. By providing suitable habitat and food sources, you create an environment where these insects can thrive and contribute to garden health.

8. Respect Wildlife Habits: Respect the natural habits and behaviors of wildlife. Avoid disrupting nesting sites, hibernation spots, or natural habitats. Keep a safe distance and observe wildlife without causing undue stress or harm.

CHAPTER 10 PESTS AND INSECTS

By respecting their space, you foster a harmonious coexistence that benefits both the wildlife and your garden.

9. Native Trees for Birds: Plant native trees that provide food and nesting opportunities for birds. Examples include oaks, birches, dogwoods, and fruit-bearing trees like cherry or serviceberry. Trees offer shade, shelter, and nesting sites, attracting a variety of bird species that can assist in pest control and contribute to the overall biodiversity of your garden.
10. Observe and Learn: Take time to observe the wildlife in your garden and learn about their habits and interactions. This not only deepens your appreciation for the natural world but also helps you understand the role each creature plays in the garden ecosystem. By observing wildlife, you can make informed choices to further enhance their presence and contributions in your garden.

Remember, a garden teeming with wildlife is a garden in balance. By respecting and attracting beneficial wildlife, you create a symbiotic relationship that supports a healthy and thriving garden ecosystem. Enjoy the beauty of nature and embrace the invaluable assistance provided by your garden's wildlife allies.

#74 Install a birdbath: Birds will help control pests in your garden.

The Birdbath Hack: Inviting Nature's Song and Beauty

Installing a birdbath in your garden not only adds an enchanting focal point but also provides numerous advantages for both birds and your garden ecosystem. It's a simple and effective way to attract feathered friends, promote biodiversity, and enhance the overall beauty of your outdoor space. Here's why installing a birdbath is a fantastic gardening hack:

1. Water Source for Birds: Birds need a reliable water source for drinking, bathing, and preening their feathers. By installing a birdbath, you offer a refreshing oasis that attracts a variety of bird species to your garden. The sight and sound of birds splashing and fluttering in the water adds a delightful touch of liveliness and serenity to your outdoor environment.
2. Encourages Bird Diversity: Birds are drawn to water, and a birdbath acts as a magnet, attracting different species to your garden. By providing a birdbath, you create an opportunity to observe a variety of birds up close and enjoy their diverse colors, patterns, and behaviors. This enriches your garden experience and deepens your connection with nature.
3. Natural Pest Control: Many bird species are voracious insect eaters and play a crucial role in natural pest control. By attracting birds to your garden through a birdbath, you create a balanced ecosystem where they actively seek out and consume garden pests like caterpillars, aphids, and beetles. Birds help reduce pest populations naturally, reducing the need for chemical interventions.
4. Pollination Assistance: Birds, particularly hummingbirds, play a vital role in pollination. While they primarily seek nectar from flowers, a birdbath offers them a nearby water source to replenish their energy after foraging. As they visit your birdbath, they inadvertently transfer pollen from flower to flower, aiding in the pollination process and promoting fruit set in your garden.

5. Year-Round Beauty: A birdbath adds visual appeal and year-round beauty to your garden. Even when flowers are not in bloom, a well-designed birdbath becomes a focal point, attracting attention with its elegant design and the playful interactions of visiting birds. Enhance the beauty by incorporating decorative elements like stones, shells, or floating flowers.
6. Peaceful Ambience: The sound of flowing or splashing water creates a calming and soothing atmosphere in your garden. The gentle gurgling or chirping sounds of birds enjoying the birdbath contribute to a peaceful ambiance, providing a tranquil space for relaxation, meditation, or simply enjoying the wonders of nature.
7. Educational Opportunity: A birdbath offers an educational opportunity for all ages. Observing birds up close and learning about their behaviors, migration patterns, and unique characteristics can foster a deeper appreciation and understanding of the natural world. It provides a chance to connect with children or visitors and instill a love for wildlife and conservation.
8. Low Maintenance: Birdbaths are relatively low-maintenance garden features. Ensure the birdbath is kept clean and the water is refreshed regularly to prevent stagnation and maintain hygiene. A shallow birdbath is ideal to allow birds to bathe safely. Consider adding a small pump or fountain feature to keep the water moving, reducing the risk of mosquito breeding.
9. Aesthetic Integration: A well-placed birdbath can be seamlessly integrated into your garden design. Choose a location that offers visibility from both inside and outside your home, allowing you to enjoy the bird activity through-

out the seasons. Consider surrounding the birdbath with native plants or a small seating area to create a welcoming space for both birds and garden visitors.
10. Environmental Connection: Installing a birdbath fosters a deeper connection with the natural environment and reminds us of the interconnectedness of all living beings. It encourages us to appreciate the beauty and intricacies of the avian world, inspiring us to make conscious choices that promote biodiversity, conservation, and the preservation of our natural heritage.

By installing a birdbath, you create a captivating focal point that welcomes birds, supports biodiversity, and adds an enchanting touch to your garden. Embrace the advantages of a birdbath and relish the harmonious interactions between birds and your garden ecosystem.

#75 Attract birds: Install bird feeders to attract birds, which can help control pests.
The Bird Feeder Hack: Inviting Nature's Chorus to Your Garden
Installing bird feeders in your garden is an effective way to attract a diverse array of birds, providing numerous benefits for both the birds and your garden ecosystem. It's a simple and enjoyable gardening hack that enhances the beauty of your outdoor space while nurturing a thriving avian community. Here's why installing bird feeders is a fantastic addition to your garden:

1. Food and Nutritional Support: Bird feeders offer a supplemental food source for birds, especially during periods

CHAPTER 10 PESTS AND INSECTS

of natural food scarcity, such as winter or dry seasons. By providing a reliable supply of bird-friendly seeds, nuts, or suet, you help sustain birds throughout the year. This support is particularly crucial during migration or breeding seasons when birds require extra energy.

2. Attracts a Variety of Bird Species: Different bird species have varied feeding preferences. By offering a variety of bird feeders and food options, you can attract a diverse range of birds to your garden. Each species brings its unique colors, patterns, songs, and behaviors, creating a vibrant tapestry of nature's beauty right outside your window.

3. Educational and Entertainment Value: Bird feeders provide an exciting opportunity for observation and learning. Set up feeders near a window or outdoor seating area where you can easily observe the feeding habits, interactions, and social dynamics of visiting birds. This engaging experience offers educational value for children and adults alike, fostering a deeper understanding and appreciation for the avian world.

4. Natural Pest Control: Many birds are natural predators of garden pests, including insects, slugs, and snails. By attracting birds to your garden through bird feeders, you create an environment where they actively seek out and consume harmful pests. Birds play a crucial role in maintaining the ecological balance of your garden, reducing the need for chemical pesticides.

5. Pollination Assistance: Some bird species, such as hummingbirds, are important pollinators. By providing nectar-rich feeders or planting hummingbird-friendly flowers nearby, you encourage these avian pollinators

to visit your garden. As they feed on nectar, they inadvertently transfer pollen from flower to flower, promoting pollination and fruit production in your garden.
6. Year-Round Beauty: Bird feeders add year-round beauty and activity to your garden landscape. Even in the absence of blooming flowers, the sight of birds fluttering around the feeders brings life, color, and joy to your outdoor space. Their vibrant plumage and melodious songs enrich the visual and auditory appeal of your garden throughout the seasons.
7. Seed Dispersal and Seed-Saving: Birds assist in seed dispersion as they feed on seeds and berries. By attracting birds to your garden through feeders, they may consume seeds from plants that self-sow or produce seeds beneficial for regrowth in the following seasons. This natural process helps maintain biodiversity and supports the continuation of plant species in your garden.
8. Emotional Well-being: Observing birds and connecting with nature has been shown to have positive effects on emotional well-being, reducing stress and promoting relaxation. The presence of birds and their melodious songs can create a soothing ambiance that brings a sense of peace and tranquility to your garden space.
9. Predator Alert System: Birds are naturally cautious and sensitive to predators in the environment. Their presence in your garden acts as a built-in alert system, notifying other wildlife of potential threats like cats or larger birds of prey. This can help protect smaller garden inhabitants like songbirds, rabbits, or beneficial insects.
10. Conservation and Environmental Awareness: By

CHAPTER 10 PESTS AND INSECTS

installing bird feeders, you contribute to conservation efforts by supporting local bird populations and raising environmental awareness. You become an active participant in preserving biodiversity and promoting a healthier ecosystem within your community.

Installing bird feeders in your garden invites a symphony of birds, fostering a deeper connection with nature and providing numerous benefits to your garden ecosystem. Enjoy the beauty, entertainment, and ecological value that these feathered visitors bring to your outdoor space.

#76 Plant herbs to repel pests: Certain herbs, like mint and basil, can repel pests.

The Pest-Repelling Herb Hack: Natural Protection for Your Garden

Planting herbs with pest-repelling properties in your garden is an effective and natural way to deter pests without relying on chemical pesticides. These aromatic herbs emit scents that act as natural repellents, keeping harmful insects at bay and protecting your plants. Here's how to make the most of pest-repelling herbs in your garden:

1. Choose the Right Herbs: Select herbs that have proven pest-repelling properties. Examples include:

- Basil: Repels flies, mosquitoes, and aphids.
- Lavender: Deters fleas, moths, and mosquitoes.
- Rosemary: Repels cabbage moths, carrot flies, and mosquitoes.
- Mint: Deters ants, aphids, and cabbage moths.

- Thyme: Repels whiteflies, cabbage worms, and slugs.
- Chives: Deter aphids, Japanese beetles, and carrot flies.

1. Interplant Herbs Throughout the Garden: Integrate pest-repelling herbs throughout your garden beds or in containers. Plant them near susceptible plants to create a protective barrier. By intermingling these herbs, you can confuse pests with their strong scents and make it more challenging for them to locate their preferred host plants.
2. Introduce Companion Planting: Incorporate herbs with pest-repelling properties as companion plants for susceptible vegetables, flowers, or herbs. For example, plant basil near tomatoes to deter tomato hornworms, or place lavender near roses to repel aphids. The aromatic presence of these herbs helps shield neighboring plants from pests.
3. Utilize Herb Bouquets: Harvest your pest-repelling herbs and use them to create herb bouquets or arrangements. Place these bouquets near windows, entryways, or outdoor seating areas to naturally deter flying insects like flies and mosquitoes.
4. Crush and Scatter Herb Leaves: Crush the leaves of your pest-repelling herbs to release their strong scents. Scatter the crushed leaves around your garden beds, focusing on areas prone to pest infestations. This creates a natural barrier and increases the scent intensity, deterring pests from approaching your plants.
5. Create Herbal Sprays: Make homemade herbal sprays by infusing the leaves of pest-repelling herbs in water. Strain the liquid, pour it into a spray bottle, and spritz it on vulnerable plants. This acts as a natural repellent and can help deter pests like aphids, caterpillars, or beetles.

Experiment with different herbal combinations to find what works best for your garden.
6. Harvest and Dry Herbs: Regularly harvest your pest-repelling herbs and dry them for later use. The dried herbs can be used to create sachets or bundles that repel pests indoors or in storage areas where you store harvested produce or garden supplies.
7. Consider Container Gardening: If you have limited space or want greater control over your herb plantings, consider growing pest-repelling herbs in containers. This allows you to easily move them around your garden, patio, or balcony, targeting specific areas or plants that require protection from pests.
8. Be Mindful of Growth Habits: Keep in mind that some pest-repelling herbs, such as mint or lemon balm, can be vigorous spreaders. To prevent them from becoming invasive, consider planting them in containers or confining their growth by burying the pot in the soil, leaving the rim aboveground.
9. Regular Maintenance: To maximize the pest-repelling effects of your herbs, ensure proper maintenance. Trim back overgrown herbs to promote healthy growth and release fresh scents. Remove any damaged or diseased foliage promptly to prevent attracting pests or compromising the overall health of your garden.

By incorporating pest-repelling herbs into your garden, you create a naturally fortified space that wards off unwanted pests. Enjoy the beauty, aroma, and protective benefits these herbs provide while cultivating a thriving and pest-resistant garden.

#77 Create a homemade bug spray: A mixture of dish soap and water can help get rid of aphids.

The Homemade Aphid Spray Hack: Simple and Effective Aphid Control

Aphids can quickly become a nuisance in the garden, damaging plants and hindering their growth. This homemade aphid spray is a cost-effective and natural solution that helps eliminate aphids without resorting to harsh chemicals. Here's how to create and use the spray effectively:

Ingredients:

- 1 tablespoon mild liquid dish soap (avoid using soap with added fragrance or antibacterial properties)
- 1 quart (4 cups) of water
- Spray bottle

Instructions:

1. Fill a spray bottle with 1 quart (4 cups) of water. Ensure the bottle is clean and free of any residue from previous chemicals or solutions.
2. Add 1 tablespoon of mild liquid dish soap to the water. Gently swirl the bottle to mix the soap with the water. Avoid shaking vigorously to prevent excessive foaming.

Application:

1. Identify the areas affected by aphids. These may include the undersides of leaves, new growth, or densely populated areas.
2. Test the spray on a small section of the plant to check for

any adverse reactions. Some delicate or sensitive plants may react negatively to the soap solution.
3. Once confirmed, spray the homemade aphid spray directly onto the affected plants, targeting the aphids and the areas where they congregate.
4. Ensure thorough coverage of the aphids, focusing on the undersides of leaves where they often hide.
5. Repeat the application every few days or as needed until the aphids are under control.

Tips:

- Apply the spray during cooler hours of the day, preferably in the morning or evening, to prevent potential leaf burn caused by the sun's intensity.
- Use a fine mist setting on your spray bottle for better coverage and distribution of the homemade spray.
- For heavily infested plants, consider physically removing the aphids by gently wiping or spraying them off with water before applying the homemade spray. This can help enhance the effectiveness of the treatment.
- Monitor the plants regularly and reapply the spray if necessary, especially after rainfall.

Why It Works:

The soap in the spray disrupts the waxy protective coating on aphids' bodies, causing them to dehydrate and perish. Additionally, the soapy solution coats the aphids and suffocates them, making it difficult for them to breathe and feed on your plants.

Note:

While this homemade aphid spray is effective against aphids, it may also affect beneficial insects. To minimize harm to beneficial insects, focus the spray directly on the aphids and avoid drenching the entire plant unless necessary. Consider using this spray in a targeted manner or applying it only when aphid infestations are severe.

By using this simple homemade aphid spray, you can naturally and effectively control aphids in your garden, promoting the health and vitality of your plants without resorting to harsh chemicals.

#78 Use beer to trap slugs: A little beer in a shallow container can attract and drown slugs.

Gardening Hack: Slug Trap with Beer

Are pesky slugs wreaking havoc on your garden, munching away at your precious plants? Worry no more! This simple and effective gardening hack will help you control those slimy intruders using an unlikely ally: beer.

Here's how you can use beer to trap slugs and protect your beloved plants:

1. Select a container: Choose a shallow container, such as a small bowl or saucer, that is wide enough to accommodate slugs.
2. Bury the container: Dig a small hole in the ground near the affected plants, making sure the rim of the container is level with the soil surface.
3. Fill the container with beer: Pour some beer into the container, filling it up about halfway. Slugs are attracted to the scent of beer and will be lured into the trap.

4. Create a shelter: To enhance the effectiveness of the trap, place a board or a piece of wood over the container. This creates a dark and moist environment that slugs find irresistible.
5. Check the trap daily: Slugs are most active during the evening and nighttime, so be sure to check the trap early in the morning. You'll likely find slugs that have fallen into the beer and are unable to escape.
6. Dispose of the slugs: Once you've caught the slugs, remove them from the trap and dispose of them responsibly. You can either relocate them away from your garden or eliminate them using environmentally friendly methods.

Why does this gardening hack work? Slugs are attracted to the yeast in beer and are lured into the container. Once they crawl in, they are unable to escape due to the slippery surface of the beer. This natural and non-toxic method helps to reduce slug populations without the use of harmful chemicals.

Remember to replenish the beer as needed to keep the trap effective. Additionally, keep the area surrounding the trap free of debris and plant matter, as this can provide alternative hiding spots for slugs.

With this simple beer trap, you can protect your plants from the voracious appetites of slugs while avoiding the use of harmful pesticides. Enjoy a slug-free garden and the satisfaction of knowing you've outsmarted those slimy garden pests.

Cheers to a beautiful and pest-free garden!

#79 Use a plastic fork to deter critters: Place plastic forks prongs-up around your plants to deter rabbits and other small animals.

Gardening Hack: Plastic Forks to Deter Critters

Are critters wreaking havoc on your garden, munching on your precious plants? Don't let them get the upper hand! This simple and cost-effective gardening hack will help you protect your garden from unwanted visitors using a surprising tool: plastic forks.

Here's how you can use plastic forks to deter critters and safeguard your plants:

1. Gather plastic forks: Collect a handful of plastic forks. Opt for the disposable kind, as they are readily available and budget-friendly.
2. Insert forks around your garden: Take the plastic forks and push them into the soil around the perimeter of your garden beds or individual plants. Place them with the prongs facing upward and at a slight angle.
3. Create a barrier: The forks act as a physical barrier, making it difficult for critters like squirrels, rabbits, or even cats to navigate through your garden. The prongs deter them from stepping on or digging around your plants.
4. Maintain spacing: Space the plastic forks closely together, leaving no gaps for critters to squeeze through. This reinforces the deterrent effect and provides comprehensive coverage for your plants.
5. Monitor and adjust: Regularly check your garden and ensure the forks remain in place. Adjust them if necessary or insert additional forks where critters are attempting to breach your defenses.

Why does this gardening hack work? Critters find the sensation

CHAPTER 10 PESTS AND INSECTS

of the fork prongs unpleasant on their paws or claws, deterring them from venturing further into your garden. This humane and eco-friendly method helps protect your plants without causing harm to animals.

The plastic forks also serve as a visual deterrent, signaling to critters that your garden is off-limits. They are a low-cost alternative to more elaborate or expensive animal-repellent solutions, and you can reuse them season after season.

Remember, this gardening hack works best as part of a multi-pronged approach to critter control. Combine it with other strategies like fencing, companion planting, and proper garden maintenance for optimal results.

With plastic forks strategically placed around your garden, you can create a barrier that discourages critters from snacking on your plants. Enjoy the fruits of your labor without sharing them with unwelcome visitors.

So, gather those plastic forks, roll up your sleeves, and take control of your garden's defenses. Protect your plants and outsmart the critters with this simple, effective, and budget-friendly gardening hack.

Happy gardening and critter-free harvests!

#80 Use chamomile tea on seedlings: It can prevent damping off disease.

Gardening Hack: Chamomile Tea to Prevent Damping Off Disease in Seedlings

Damping off disease can be a frustrating setback for any gardener, causing seedlings to wither and die before they even have a chance to thrive. But fear not! This simple and natural gardening hack using chamomile tea can help prevent damping off and give your seedlings the best start possible.

Here's how you can use chamomile tea to protect your seedlings from damping off disease:

1. Brew chamomile tea: Start by brewing a pot of chamomile tea using organic chamomile tea bags or dried chamomile flowers. Follow the instructions on the package to make a strong infusion.
2. Let the tea cool: Allow the chamomile tea to cool completely. It's essential not to use hot tea, as it can harm delicate seedlings.
3. Transfer tea to a spray bottle: Pour the cooled chamomile tea into a clean spray bottle for easy application.
4. Mist the seedlings: Gently mist the seedlings with the chamomile tea, making sure to cover the stems and surrounding soil. The natural compounds found in chamomile have antifungal properties that help combat damping off disease.
5. Repeat as needed: Apply the chamomile tea spray once every few days or after watering to maintain its protective effect. Continue this practice until the seedlings have grown stronger and are less susceptible to damping off.

Why does this gardening hack work? Chamomile tea contains natural compounds, including chamazulene, which possess antifungal properties. When applied to the seedlings, the chamomile tea forms a protective barrier, inhibiting the growth of damping off pathogens.

Remember, prevention is key when it comes to damping off disease. Along with using chamomile tea, ensure proper seedling hygiene, provide adequate air circulation, and avoid overwatering to create an unfavorable environment for fungal growth.

By incorporating chamomile tea into your seedling care routine, you can give your young plants a fighting chance against damping off disease. Enjoy healthy and vigorous seedlings that will grow into thriving plants in your garden.

Cheers to the power of chamomile and successful gardening adventures!

12

Chapter 11 Weeds

#81 Know your weeds: Some weeds are harmful to your garden, but others may actually be beneficial.

The Weed ID Hack: Differentiating Harmful Weeds from Beneficial Weeds

Weeds can be a common challenge in gardening, but not all weeds are created equal. Some weeds can actually provide benefits to your garden ecosystem, while others can harm your plants and compete for resources. Here's how to identify harmful weeds from beneficial weeds:

1. Educate Yourself: Take the time to educate yourself about common weeds in your region. Learn to recognize their distinctive features, growth habits, and potential impact on your garden. Local gardening resources, books, or online weed identification guides specific to your area can be valuable references.
2. Observe Growth Habits: Pay attention to the growth habits of different weeds. Harmful weeds often spread

rapidly and aggressively, smothering desirable plants and competing for nutrients, light, and water. Beneficial weeds, on the other hand, tend to have more controlled growth and may even provide ecological benefits like soil improvement or attracting beneficial insects.

3. Know the Life Cycle: Understand the life cycle of different weeds. Annual weeds complete their life cycle in one growing season, while perennial weeds persist and regrow from roots or underground structures. Annual weeds tend to be easier to control as they germinate from seeds each year, while perennial weeds require more consistent management to prevent their spread.

4. Identify Harmful Weeds: Look out for common harmful weeds that can invade your garden and cause problems. These may include aggressive grasses like crabgrass or quackgrass, invasive vines such as bindweed or English ivy, or plants with thorny or prickly structures like thistles. These weeds often outcompete desired plants and can be challenging to eradicate once established.

5. Recognize Beneficial Weeds: Some weeds can have beneficial properties in the garden. For example, clover can fix nitrogen in the soil, dandelions provide early food sources for pollinators, and purslane offers edible leaves rich in omega-3 fatty acids. These weeds can be tolerated or even intentionally incorporated into your garden design, as long as they don't become invasive or overpower desirable plants.

6. Consider Context and Location: Evaluate the location and context of the weed. Weeds that emerge in open areas of your garden bed where you have yet to plant desired plants may be easier to remove or manage. However, weeds that

emerge among delicate or established plants may require more careful and targeted weed control methods.
7. Implement Weed Control Strategies: Once you've identified harmful weeds, develop a weed control strategy tailored to each specific weed. This may involve techniques such as hand-pulling, mulching, smothering with organic materials, or targeted use of organic herbicides. For beneficial weeds, monitor their growth and take preventive measures to prevent them from becoming invasive or detrimental to your garden.
8. Regular Maintenance: Stay proactive with regular garden maintenance practices to minimize weed growth. These include timely weeding, mulching to suppress weed germination, practicing good soil health, and providing optimal growing conditions for your desired plants. A well-maintained garden is less likely to be overtaken by weeds.

Remember, weed management is an ongoing process, and it's essential to strike a balance between controlling harmful weeds and appreciating the benefits of beneficial weeds. By developing your weed identification skills and implementing effective weed control strategies, you can maintain a healthier and more thriving garden.

#82 Control weeds: Hand-pulling is a safe and sure way to get rid of weeds.

The Hand-Pulling Weed Control Hack: Tackling Weeds Naturally

Hand-pulling weeds is an effective and environmentally friendly method to control weeds in your garden. It allows you to directly target and remove unwanted plants, reducing competition for resources and promoting the health of your desired plants. Here's how to make the most of hand-pulling for weed control:

1. Timing is Key: Pull weeds when they are young and small. Young weeds have shallow root systems and are easier to uproot entirely. Aim to remove them before they have a chance to produce seeds or establish a stronger foothold in your garden.
2. Prepare the Soil: Before you start hand-pulling, moisten the soil slightly to loosen it and make weed removal easier. This is particularly helpful when dealing with stubborn or deep-rooted weeds. Avoid watering excessively, as it may make the soil muddy and difficult to work with.
3. Use the Right Tools: Equip yourself with appropriate tools for effective weed removal. A hand trowel, garden fork, or weed puller can be useful for different types of weeds and soil conditions. Choose a tool that allows you to grasp the weed close to the base and apply gentle leverage to extract it entirely.
4. Grasp the Weed Properly: To ensure successful removal, grip the weed as close to the base as possible, near the soil line. This helps prevent the weed from breaking off, leaving behind the roots to regenerate. Firmly but gently pull the weed upwards, ensuring that you extract the entire plant, including the roots.
5. Dispose of Weeds Properly: Once you've pulled the weeds, promptly remove them from your garden to prevent reseeding or reestablishment. Place them in a designated compost pile, if appropriate, or dispose of them in a way

that prevents them from spreading seeds or regrowing in unwanted areas.
6. Regular Inspections: Regularly inspect your garden beds for emerging weeds. Catching weeds early and pulling them promptly reduces the effort required for control and minimizes their impact on your desired plants. Make hand-pulling a part of your routine garden maintenance to stay ahead of weed growth.
7. Mulch for Weed Suppression: After hand-pulling weeds, consider applying a layer of organic mulch, such as wood chips or straw, around your plants. Mulching helps suppress weed germination and growth by creating a barrier that limits sunlight and access to the soil surface.
8. Consistency is Key: Weed control through hand-pulling requires consistency and ongoing effort. Regularly dedicate time to inspecting and tending to your garden, pulling weeds as soon as they appear. By consistently removing weeds before they become established, you reduce the likelihood of larger weed populations and lessen the impact on your desired plants.
9. Preventive Measures: Implement preventive measures to reduce future weed growth. This includes techniques such as applying pre-emergent herbicides or using landscape fabric or cardboard as a weed barrier before planting new garden beds. Preventing weed seeds from reaching the soil surface helps minimize future weed challenges.
10. Patience and Persistence: Hand-pulling weeds may take time and effort, but it's a natural and effective method of weed control. Embrace the process, view it as an opportunity to connect with your garden, and appreciate the satisfaction of maintaining a weed-free and thriving

garden space.

By incorporating hand-pulling as a regular practice in your gardening routine, you can effectively control weeds without relying on chemicals or herbicides. It allows you to target weeds directly, promoting the health of your desired plants and creating a more beautiful and harmonious garden environment.

#83 Weed regularly: Weeds compete with your plants for nutrients and water. Keep them under control.

The Regular Weeding Hack: Nurturing a Weed-Free Garden

Regular weeding is a fundamental practice that promotes the health and beauty of your garden. It allows your desired plants to thrive by reducing competition for resources and minimizing the negative impacts of weeds. By incorporating regular weeding into your garden routine, you'll enjoy a more vibrant and flourishing garden. Here's why regular weeding is essential:

1. Resource Competition: Weeds compete with your desired plants for essential resources such as water, nutrients, sunlight, and space. They can deprive your plants of the resources they need to grow, leading to stunted growth, reduced vigor, and lower yields. Regular weeding ensures that your plants have unhindered access to the resources they require for optimal health and productivity.
2. Preventing Weed Spread: Weeds are prolific seed producers, and if left unchecked, they can quickly multiply and spread throughout your garden. Regular weeding interrupts the life cycle of weeds, preventing them from going to seed and dispersing more weed seeds. By remov-

ing weeds before they have a chance to reproduce, you significantly reduce future weed problems.

3. Aesthetics and Garden Beauty: A weed-free garden is visually appealing and showcases the beauty of your carefully chosen plants. Regular weeding helps maintain a tidy and well-groomed appearance, enhancing the overall aesthetics of your garden. It allows your plants to shine and take center stage without being overshadowed by unsightly and invasive weeds.

4. Preventing Weed Smothering: Some weeds, such as fast-growing and aggressive vines or groundcovers, have the potential to smother and suffocate your desired plants. They can overtake garden beds, climb trellises, or cover the soil surface, outcompeting and suppressing your plants. Regular weeding prevents weeds from smothering and weakening your garden plants.

5. Disease and Pest Reduction: Weeds can harbor pests and diseases, providing a favorable environment for their growth and spread. By removing weeds promptly, you reduce the risk of these pests and diseases finding refuge in your garden. Regular weeding, combined with good garden hygiene practices, creates an inhospitable environment for pests and helps maintain a healthier garden ecosystem.

6. Reducing Maintenance Time: Addressing weeds early and consistently through regular weeding helps reduce the overall maintenance time in your garden. By removing weeds while they are small and easier to control, you prevent them from establishing deep root systems or spreading extensively. This saves you time and effort in the long run, as larger and more established weeds can be

more challenging to eradicate.
7. Enhancing Plant Diversity: Regular weeding contributes to a more diverse garden ecosystem by reducing the dominance of invasive and opportunistic weeds. It allows space for a wider range of desirable plants, including flowers, vegetables, herbs, or native species, to flourish and contribute to a more balanced and resilient garden environment.
8. Connecting with Your Garden: Regular weeding provides an opportunity to connect with your garden on a deeper level. It allows you to observe the health and progress of your plants, notice any signs of stress or disease, and appreciate the intricate details of growth and development. Weeding can be a meditative and satisfying activity that promotes mindfulness and a stronger bond with your garden space.
9. Weeding as Preventive Care: Regular weeding is a form of preventive care for your garden. By addressing weeds early and consistently, you reduce the likelihood of severe weed problems that may require more aggressive and time-consuming control methods. Regular weeding is an investment in the long-term health and sustainability of your garden.
10. Environmental Stewardship: Regular weeding aligns with the principles of environmental stewardship. By managing weeds responsibly and preventing their spread, you contribute to the preservation of native plant communities, reduce the risk of invasive species encroaching on natural habitats, and create a healthier and more sustainable garden ecosystem.

By incorporating regular weeding into your garden routine, you provide a nurturing environment for your desired plants, enhance the beauty of your garden, and contribute to the overall health and sustainability of your garden ecosystem. Embrace the practice of regular weeding as a way to connect with nature, maintain a thriving garden, and enjoy the rewards of your gardening efforts.

13

Chapter 12 Tools

#84 Clean and sharp tools: This helps prevent the spread of disease in your garden.

The Clean and Sharp Tools Hack: Cultivating Efficiency and Healthy Plants

Clean and sharp gardening tools are essential for maintaining a productive and healthy garden. They not only make your gardening tasks more efficient but also contribute to the overall well-being of your plants. Incorporate the following practices to ensure your tools are clean and sharp:

1. Efficient Cutting and Pruning: Sharp tools, such as pruners, shears, and secateurs, enable clean and precise cuts, minimizing damage to plants. Clean cuts heal faster and reduce the risk of introducing diseases or infections. Regularly inspect and sharpen the cutting edges of your tools to maintain their effectiveness.
2. Preventing Disease Transmission: Cleaning your gardening tools between uses helps prevent the transmission of

diseases and pathogens from one plant to another. Wipe the blades of cutting tools with a disinfecting solution (such as rubbing alcohol or a mild bleach solution) or use dedicated tool-cleaning products. This reduces the risk of spreading diseases that can harm your plants.
3. Longevity of Tools: Keeping your tools clean and free of debris helps extend their lifespan. Remove dirt, plant sap, or other residues from the surfaces of your tools after each use. This prevents corrosion and keeps them in optimal working condition, saving you money in the long run.
4. Maintenance and Storage: Regular maintenance of your gardening tools, including cleaning, lubrication, and sharpening, ensures their proper functioning and longevity. Store them in a dry and protected area to prevent rust or damage from exposure to the elements.
5. Efficient Soil Work: Clean and sharp tools, such as shovels, hoes, and trowels, make soil preparation and cultivation easier. Sharp blades cut through soil more efficiently, reducing the effort required and providing a healthier growing environment for your plants.
6. Reducing Plant Stress: Clean and sharp pruning tools minimize stress on plants during pruning or trimming. Clean cuts heal faster, reducing the risk of diseases or pests entering through open wounds. This promotes the overall health and vitality of your plants.
7. Safety First: Clean and sharp tools are safer to use. Dull or dirty tools can slip or cause uneven cuts, increasing the risk of accidents. Regular maintenance and cleaning help ensure that your tools function properly, providing a safer gardening experience.
8. Efficiency in Garden Tasks: Clean and sharp tools make

CHAPTER 12 TOOLS

your gardening tasks more efficient. They cut through vegetation cleanly, reducing the time and effort required for trimming, pruning, or harvesting. You'll be able to work more effectively, accomplishing tasks with greater precision and less fatigue.
9. Aesthetics and Professionalism: Clean and well-maintained tools demonstrate your commitment to gardening excellence. It reflects your attention to detail and professionalism, enhancing the overall appearance and pride of your garden.
10. Enjoyment and Connection: Gardening is a fulfilling and rewarding activity. Clean and sharp tools enhance your gardening experience, allowing you to connect more deeply with your plants and the natural world. You'll experience greater satisfaction and enjoyment in tending to your garden with tools that are in optimal condition.

By incorporating regular cleaning and sharpening of your gardening tools into your routine, you cultivate efficiency, promote plant health, and enhance your overall gardening experience. Keep your tools clean, sharp, and in good working order to enjoy the benefits of efficient, safe, and enjoyable gardening.

#85 Keep a gardening journal: Note what worked and what didn't for future reference.

The Gardening Journal Hack: Cultivating Knowledge and Growth

Keeping a gardening journal is a valuable practice that allows you to track your garden's progress, learn from your experiences, and enhance your gardening skills. It serves as a personal record of your gardening journey and provides a wealth of information that can help you make informed decisions and improve your gardening outcomes. Here's why keeping a gardening journal is so important:

1. Track Planting and Harvesting Dates: Recording the dates when you sow seeds, transplant seedlings, or harvest crops helps you establish a timeline for future reference. It provides valuable insights into the timing and success of your gardening efforts, helping you plan and adjust your planting schedule in subsequent seasons.
2. Document Plant Performance: Note the performance of different plants in your garden. Record growth rates, flowering or fruiting patterns, disease resistance, and overall health. This information helps you identify which plants thrive in your specific garden conditions, allowing you to make informed choices for future plantings.
3. Record Garden Observations: Use your journal to note important observations about your garden. Document weather patterns, pest and disease occurrences, and any specific challenges or successes you encounter. This information helps you identify patterns and trends, enabling you to implement proactive measures to address issues or replicate successful practices.
4. Capture Gardening Techniques: Jot down gardening techniques, tips, and tricks you learn along the way. These can include soil amendments, pruning methods, companion planting strategies, or pest control approaches. By documenting these techniques in your journal, you create a personalized knowledge base that you can refer to for future gardening endeavors.

5. Experimentation and Success Tracking: Use your journal to record any gardening experiments you undertake. Note the techniques, variables, and outcomes of your experiments. This helps you assess the effectiveness of different approaches and track your gardening successes. It also provides a record of what works and what doesn't, helping you refine your gardening methods over time.
6. Plant Identification and Descriptions: Include detailed information about the plants in your garden. Record the names, varieties, and specific characteristics of each plant. This information serves as a helpful reference, especially when you want to replicate successful plantings or share gardening advice with others.
7. Garden Design and Layout: Sketch or draw garden layouts and design ideas in your journal. Document the placement of different plants, structures, or features. This helps you visualize and plan your garden spaces, ensuring efficient use of available resources and creating aesthetically pleasing arrangements.
8. Problem-Solving and Troubleshooting: Use your journal to document gardening challenges and the solutions you implement. This allows you to track and learn from your problem-solving experiences. By referring back to your journal, you can quickly find strategies that worked well in the past when faced with similar issues.
9. Personal Reflection and Inspiration: Your gardening journal is a personal space where you can reflect on your experiences, express your thoughts, and draw inspiration. Use it to capture the joy, surprises, and lessons you learn along your gardening journey. Reviewing your journal can ignite creativity, motivate you to try new things, and

rekindle your passion for gardening.

10. A Legacy of Knowledge: Your gardening journal becomes a precious record of your gardening endeavors. It can be passed down to future generations, offering a treasure trove of gardening knowledge, personal anecdotes, and cherished memories. It serves as a living legacy, inspiring others to continue the gardening tradition with the wisdom you have accumulated.

By keeping a gardening journal, you cultivate a deeper understanding of your garden, gain valuable insights, and foster continuous growth as a gardener. Embrace this practice and watch your gardening skills flourish as you create a personalized repository of knowledge and experiences.

#86 Learn from others: Join a local gardening club or online forum to learn from experienced gardeners.

The Learning Community Hack: Tapping into Gardening Wisdom

Joining a local gardening club or participating in online gardening forums opens up a world of knowledge and experience beyond your own garden. Connecting with fellow gardeners allows you to learn from their successes and challenges, gain new perspectives, and expand your gardening expertise. Here's why engaging with a gardening community is so important:

1. Shared Knowledge and Expertise: Gardening communities provide a wealth of collective knowledge and expertise. By joining a local gardening club or participating in online forums, you gain access to a vast network of experienced gardeners who can offer valuable insights, tips, and guid-

ance. Learning from others' experiences can save you time, effort, and potential frustrations.
2. Plant Recommendations and Varieties: Gardening communities are excellent sources for plant recommendations and introductions to new plant varieties. Fellow gardeners can share their favorite plant selections, reliable varieties for your region, and suggestions for plants that thrive in specific conditions. This helps you discover exciting and well-suited plants that you may not have encountered otherwise.
3. Regional Gardening Advice: Local gardening clubs provide region-specific advice tailored to your unique climate, soil conditions, and challenges. Fellow gardeners who are familiar with your area can offer insights into local gardening practices, pest control methods, and suitable planting times. This specialized knowledge helps you make informed decisions and increases your chances of gardening success.
4. Problem-Solving Support: Gardening communities offer a supportive environment for troubleshooting gardening problems. When faced with challenges such as pest infestations, diseases, or plant issues, fellow gardeners can provide advice, suggest solutions, and offer encouragement. Sharing your own experiences can also contribute to the collective knowledge of the community.
5. Inspiration and Ideas: Engaging with a gardening community provides an endless source of inspiration and ideas for your garden. Seeing photographs, hearing success stories, and learning about innovative gardening techniques from other members can spark creativity and expand your gardening horizons. You may discover new plants, design

concepts, or sustainable practices that invigorate your gardening endeavors.

6. Seed and Plant Swaps: Gardening communities often organize seed and plant swaps, allowing you to acquire unique and diverse plant material at minimal or no cost. Exchanging seeds or plants with fellow gardeners not only broadens your plant collection but also cultivates a sense of community and fosters biodiversity in your garden.

7. Camaraderie and Social Connections: Joining a gardening club or participating in online forums connects you with like-minded individuals who share your passion for gardening. Building relationships with fellow gardeners provides a sense of camaraderie, allows you to exchange stories and experiences, and fosters lasting friendships. Gardening becomes a shared journey that brings people together.

8. Continuous Learning and Growth: Engaging with a gardening community promotes continuous learning and growth as a gardener. By staying connected and actively participating in discussions, you remain up to date with the latest gardening trends, techniques, and research. You can expand your gardening skills, experiment with new approaches, and stay inspired to try new things.

9. Community Projects and Events: Gardening communities often organize community projects, garden tours, workshops, or educational events. Participating in these activities not only deepens your gardening knowledge but also contributes to the broader gardening community. You have the opportunity to give back, share your own expertise, and inspire fellow gardeners.

10. A Sense of Belonging: By joining a gardening club or en-

gaging in online forums, you become part of a gardening family. You share a common interest and a love for plants and nature. This sense of belonging fosters a supportive and inclusive environment where you can freely share your joys, challenges, and accomplishments with fellow gardeners.

By actively participating in a local gardening club or online gardening forum, you tap into a vast reservoir of gardening wisdom, forge meaningful connections, and foster continuous learning. Embrace the power of community, and watch your gardening skills and enjoyment flourish with the collective knowledge and support of fellow gardeners.

#87 Provide supports: Plants like tomatoes, beans, and peas need stakes or cages for support.
The Plant Support Hack: Growing Upwards for Thriving Crops
Providing adequate support for your climbing plants, such as tomatoes, beans, and peas, is essential for their healthy growth, maximized yields, and easier maintenance. By incorporating plant supports, you'll create a vertical growing space, save garden space, and prevent sprawling or damage to your crops. Here's how to effectively support tomatoes, beans, and peas:
1. Tomato Cages or Stakes:

- Tomato Cages: Use commercial or homemade tomato cages, typically made of sturdy wire or metal. Place the cage around the tomato plant at the time of planting, ensuring it reaches the desired height.
- Stakes: Insert tall stakes (bamboo, wood, or metal) into

the ground near the base of the tomato plant. As the plant grows, loosely tie the main stem to the stake using soft plant ties or twine. Add additional ties along the stem for extra support.

2. Trellises or A-Frames for Beans:

- Trellises: Set up trellises or wire mesh panels along the row of beans. Ensure the trellis is tall enough to accommodate the height of the bean plants. As the plants grow, gently train them to climb the trellis, using soft ties if needed.
- A-Frames: Create A-shaped frames using bamboo poles or other sturdy materials. Place them at each end of the row, with the tops joined together. Secure the frame with twine or zip ties. Plant beans along the base of each A-frame and guide the plants to grow upwards as they climb the frame.

3. Teepees or Trellises for Peas:

- Teepees: Construct teepee-shaped structures using bamboo poles, wooden stakes, or sturdy branches. Arrange them in a circular formation, leaving enough space between each pole for air circulation. Tie the tops of the poles together, forming a cone shape. Plant peas at the base of each pole, guiding them to climb the teepee structure as they grow.
- Trellises: Install trellises or wire mesh panels vertically in the garden bed. Plant peas at the base of the trellis, and as the plants grow, gently train them to climb the trellis by loosely tying the tendrils or using plant clips to secure them.

CHAPTER 12 TOOLS

Tips for Effective Plant Support:

- Install the supports early: Set up the plant supports shortly after planting to avoid disturbing the roots or damaging the plants as they grow.
- Monitor and guide growth: Regularly check the plants and gently guide their growth by securing stems or tendrils to the supports as needed. This helps prevent breakage and ensures proper alignment.
- Use soft ties or twine: To avoid damaging the stems, use soft plant ties, twine, or strips of fabric to secure plants to the supports. Check and adjust the ties periodically to accommodate the plant's growth.
- Train plants early: Encourage the plants to climb the supports by gently redirecting their growth towards the desired direction. This helps prevent entanglement and allows for better air circulation and sunlight exposure.
- Adjust support height if needed: As the plants grow, you may need to adjust the height of the supports or extend them to accommodate their increasing height or length.

By providing appropriate plant supports for your tomatoes, beans, and peas, you create a vertical growing space, promote better air circulation, and make harvesting and maintenance tasks more manageable. Your plants will thrive, and you'll enjoy higher yields of delicious, homegrown produce.

#88 Stay organized: Keep your gardening tools in a specific spot so you can easily find them.
The Organized Gardener's Tool Hack: Efficiency and Ease at Your Fingertips

Staying organized with your gardening tools is crucial for maximizing efficiency, reducing frustration, and making the most of your gardening experience. By implementing organizational strategies, you'll have your tools readily available, easily accessible, and properly maintained. Here's why staying organized is important and how to achieve it:

1. Time-Saving Efficiency: Keeping your gardening tools organized saves valuable time and effort. When tools are easily accessible and well-maintained, you can quickly find what you need, eliminating unnecessary searches and delays. You'll spend less time looking for misplaced tools and more time enjoying your garden.
2. Tool Protection and Longevity: Proper organization helps protect your tools from damage and deterioration. Storing them in a designated area or toolbox prevents them from being exposed to the elements, reducing the risk of rust, corrosion, or breakage. Well-maintained tools last longer, saving you money in the long run.
3. Preventing Accidental Damage: Organized tools minimize the chance of accidental damage. By keeping sharp tools properly stored and secured, you reduce the risk of cuts or injuries. Additionally, by preventing tools from being stepped on, misplaced, or mishandled, you protect them from unnecessary wear and tear.
4. Easy Identification and Selection: An organized tool storage system allows for easy identification and selection of the right tool for the task at hand. When tools are neatly arranged and labeled, you can quickly find the tool you need without confusion or guesswork. This enhances your efficiency and ensures you have the right tool for each

gardening job.
5. Maintenance and Sharpening: Organizational systems make it easier to implement regular tool maintenance and sharpening routines. When tools are properly stored and organized, you can easily identify which ones require cleaning, oiling, or sharpening. Regular maintenance ensures that your tools function optimally and perform at their best.
6. Tool Inventory and Replacement: Maintaining an organized system helps you keep track of your tool inventory. You'll know which tools you have, which ones need replacing or upgrading, and which ones require additional care or maintenance. This allows you to make informed decisions when purchasing new tools or replacing worn-out ones.
7. Personal Safety: Organized tools contribute to a safer gardening environment. By promptly storing tools after use, you minimize the risk of tripping or falling hazards. An organized tool storage system keeps sharp or potentially dangerous tools out of reach of children or pets, ensuring a safe gardening space for everyone.
8. Peace of Mind: A well-organized tool collection provides peace of mind and reduces stress. You'll have confidence knowing that your tools are in order, ready for use, and properly maintained. This allows you to focus on the joy of gardening and relish in the beauty of your outdoor sanctuary.

Tips for Tool Organization:

- Designate a specific area: Set aside a dedicated space in your

garage, shed, or garden for tool storage. Use wall-mounted racks, pegboards, or tool hooks to keep tools organized and within reach.
- Categorize and group tools: Organize tools into categories based on their function or type. Group similar tools together, such as pruning tools, digging tools, or hand tools, for easier identification and selection.
- Label and mark: Label storage spaces or use colored tape to indicate where each tool belongs. This makes it easier to return tools to their designated spots after use.
- Clean and store properly: Before storing tools, clean off dirt or debris and ensure they are dry. Use tool-specific storage solutions, such as toolboxes, canvas tool rolls, or hanging storage bags, to keep tools protected and organized.
- Regular maintenance routine: Implement a maintenance schedule for cleaning, oiling, and sharpening tools. Keep a calendar or reminder system to ensure you stay on top of regular tool care.
- Keep an inventory list: Maintain an inventory list of your tools, noting their condition, purchase date, and any specific maintenance requirements. This helps you track your tool collection and make informed decisions when it's time for replacements or upgrades.

By staying organized with your gardening tools, you'll experience enhanced efficiency, save time and effort, and create a safer and more enjoyable gardening environment. Embrace the power of organization and elevate your gardening experience to new heights of productivity and satisfaction.

#89 Reuse coffee filters in pots: Placing a coffee filter at the bottom of a pot can prevent soil from spilling out of the drainage hole.

The Coffee Filter Hack: Enhancing Drainage and Soil Health
Coffee filters, commonly used for brewing your morning cup of joe, can also serve a useful purpose in your garden. Reusing coffee filters in pots can provide numerous benefits, including improved drainage, enhanced soil health, and easier maintenance. Here's how to incorporate coffee filters in your potted plants:

1. Enhanced Drainage: Placing a coffee filter at the bottom of a pot acts as a barrier that allows water to drain freely while preventing soil from escaping. This helps prevent waterlogging and root rot, especially in pots without drainage holes. The coffee filter acts as a filter, allowing excess water to flow out while retaining the soil.
2. Preventing Soil Erosion: Coffee filters help prevent soil erosion by keeping the soil intact in the pot. They act as a fine barrier that holds the soil in place, even during heavy watering or rainfall. This ensures that your plants' root systems remain stable and undisturbed.
3. Reduced Soil Compaction: Over time, soil in pots can become compacted, limiting root growth and nutrient absorption. By placing a coffee filter at the bottom of the pot, you create a small space that allows roots to penetrate and expand more easily. This promotes healthier root development and overall plant growth.
4. Improved Soil Moisture Retention: Coffee filters can help regulate soil moisture by acting as a water-retaining layer. They absorb excess water and release it slowly, providing a more consistent level of moisture to the soil. This is

particularly beneficial in pots where water may drain quickly, helping to maintain optimal soil moisture levels for your plants.
5. Reduced Nutrient Loss: Coffee filters help prevent nutrient loss in potted plants. As water flows through the soil, the coffee filter acts as a barrier that retains essential nutrients within the root zone. This allows plants to effectively absorb and utilize the available nutrients, promoting healthier growth and vitality.
6. Easy Cleanup: When it comes to maintenance, using coffee filters in pots makes cleanup a breeze. The filter acts as a protective layer, preventing soil from sticking to the pot's bottom and reducing the accumulation of debris. This simplifies pot cleaning and minimizes the risk of clogged drainage holes.

Tips for Using Coffee Filters in Pots:

- Choose unbleached, biodegradable coffee filters to minimize any potential environmental impact.
- Select filters that are slightly larger than the pot's drainage hole to ensure effective coverage.
- Place the coffee filter at the bottom of the pot before adding the soil, allowing it to cover the drainage holes completely.
- Avoid overwatering your potted plants, as coffee filters alone cannot compensate for excessive water usage. Always monitor soil moisture levels and water plants appropriately.

By reusing coffee filters in your pots, you can improve drainage, maintain soil health, and simplify plant care. Embrace this gardening hack to create an optimal growing environment for your potted plants and enjoy the benefits of healthier, more vibrant foliage and blooms.

#90 Install a rain gauge: This can help you understand how much extra watering your plants need.

The Rain Gauge Hack: Precise Watering and Environmental Awareness

Installing a rain gauge in your garden is a simple yet effective way to monitor rainfall levels and make informed decisions about watering your plants. By incorporating a rain gauge, you can conserve water, prevent overwatering or underwatering, and develop a deeper understanding of your garden's water needs. Here's how to install and utilize a rain gauge effectively:

1. Choose the Right Location: Select an open area in your garden that is representative of the overall rainfall in your region. Ensure that the location is free from any obstructions such as trees, buildings, or structures that could block rainfall.
2. Install at Ground Level: Position the rain gauge at ground level to capture the true amount of rainfall in your garden. Avoid placing it on elevated surfaces such as tables or platforms, as they may distort the measurements.
3. Secure the Rain Gauge: Use a stake or mount the rain gauge on a sturdy surface to keep it stable and secure. This ensures that it remains in place during rain showers or windy conditions.
4. Clear Surroundings: Clear any debris, leaves, or branches around the rain gauge to prevent obstructions that could affect accurate readings. Regularly check and clean the

rain gauge to maintain its functionality.
5. Read and Record Measurements: After rainfall events, check the rain gauge and record the measurement in a gardening journal or on a dedicated record sheet. Note the date and amount of rainfall received. This allows you to track rainfall patterns, compare measurements, and understand how it impacts your garden's watering needs.
6. Adjust Watering Practices: Use the information from your rain gauge to adjust your watering practices accordingly. If your garden receives a significant amount of rainfall, you can reduce or skip supplemental watering. On the other hand, if rainfall is scarce, you'll know when it's necessary to provide additional irrigation to support your plants' needs.
7. Promote Environmental Awareness: Monitoring rainfall through a rain gauge increases your awareness of the environment and helps you make conscious decisions about water usage. You become more connected to natural weather patterns and can contribute to water conservation efforts by optimizing irrigation practices.
8. Weather Pattern Observations: Over time, tracking rainfall measurements in your garden can reveal weather patterns and trends specific to your location. By analyzing this data, you can anticipate drought periods, prepare for heavy rainfall, and adjust your gardening plans accordingly.
9. Educational Tool for Children: Installing a rain gauge in your garden can be an educational tool for children. They can observe and participate in tracking rainfall measurements, fostering an understanding of weather, water cycles, and environmental stewardship.

10. Community Engagement: Consider participating in citizen science projects or sharing your rain gauge data with local gardening or environmental groups. Contributing to broader datasets helps researchers and fellow gardeners gain insights into regional rainfall patterns and climate variations.

By installing a rain gauge and incorporating rainfall measurements into your gardening routine, you gain valuable information that empowers you to make informed watering decisions and foster a more sustainable garden. Embrace this gardening hack to conserve water, adapt to weather patterns, and promote environmental awareness in your gardening practices.

#91 Use string to get straight planting lines: If you're planting rows or blocks, a string line can ensure they're straight.
The String Guide Hack: Achieving Straight Lines with Precision
Creating straight lines in your garden beds or for planting rows is essential for a neat and organized appearance. By utilizing a simple string guide, you can achieve precise alignment and spacing, ensuring uniformity and efficiency in your gardening tasks. Here's how to use string to get straight lines:

1. Choose a Straight Starting Point: Select a starting point where you want your straight line to begin. This could be the edge of a garden bed, a pathway, or any other fixed reference point.
2. Measure the Desired Distance: Determine the distance you want to maintain between your plants or the width of

the garden bed. Use a measuring tape or ruler to ensure accuracy.
3. Prepare the String: Cut a length of sturdy string or twine that matches the measured distance. Ensure the string is long enough to span the desired length of your straight line.
4. Secure the String: Anchor one end of the string at your starting point. You can use garden stakes, wooden dowels, or any other secure supports to keep the string in place. Insert the stakes into the ground or tie them to fixed objects, ensuring they are firmly anchored.
5. Create Tautness: Pull the string gently to create tension. Make sure it is straight and level along the desired line. Adjust the tension and alignment as needed to achieve a taut and even string.
6. Mark Your Line: Use the taut string as a guide to mark your straight line. You can use a stick, a small shovel, or your finger to create a shallow furrow in the soil along the string. This will serve as a visual reference when planting or arranging your plants.
7. Repeat as Needed: If you require multiple straight lines, reposition the string guide accordingly. Move it parallel to the initial line, ensuring consistent spacing between each line. This will help maintain uniformity in your garden beds or planting rows.

Tips for Using a String Guide:

- Use a brightly colored or contrasting string to make it more visible and easier to follow.
- Ensure the string is taut and level to achieve straight lines.

Adjust the tension and alignment as needed.
- Take measurements and mark the lines before removing the string guide to ensure accuracy.
- For longer lines or larger areas, consider using additional support stakes or intermittent guide points to maintain the string's tension and straightness.
- Store your string guide in a designated location for future use. This makes it readily accessible whenever you need to create straight lines in your garden.

By utilizing a string guide, you can achieve precise alignment, consistent spacing, and a visually appealing layout in your garden. Embrace this gardening hack to create straight lines with ease and efficiency, ensuring a well-organized and aesthetically pleasing outdoor space.

14

Chapter 13 Miscellaneous

#92 Freeze herbs in ice cube trays: If you can't use all your herbs, freeze them in water for future use in cooking.

The Herb Ice Cube Hack: Preserving Freshness and Flavor

Freezing herbs in ice cube trays is a fantastic way to preserve their freshness, flavors, and aromas for future use. By incorporating this simple technique, you can extend the lifespan of your harvested herbs, reduce waste, and have convenient herb portions ready to enhance your culinary creations. Here's how to freeze herbs in ice cube trays:

1. Harvest and Prepare Herbs: Harvest your herbs when they are at their peak freshness. Rinse them gently with water and pat them dry using a clean kitchen towel or paper towels. Remove any damaged or discolored leaves and discard any tough stems.
2. Chop or Leave Whole: Decide whether you want to freeze the herbs chopped or whole, depending on how you plan to use them in the future. Some herbs, like rosemary or

CHAPTER 13 MISCELLANEOUS

thyme, can be frozen as whole sprigs, while others, like basil or cilantro, are better chopped into smaller pieces.
3. Portion the Herbs: Fill each section of an ice cube tray with the prepared herbs. For chopped herbs, fill the sections about halfway, allowing room for expansion when freezing. For whole sprigs, place one sprig in each section, ensuring it fits comfortably.
4. Add Liquid or Olive Oil (optional): If desired, you can add a small amount of water or olive oil to the ice cube tray to help preserve the herbs and prevent freezer burn. This step is particularly useful when freezing delicate herbs like dill or parsley.
5. Freeze the Herbs: Place the ice cube tray in the freezer and allow the herbs to freeze completely. This usually takes a few hours or overnight, depending on your freezer temperature.
6. Transfer to Freezer Bags or Containers: Once the herb cubes are frozen solid, remove the ice cube tray from the freezer. Pop out the herb cubes and transfer them to freezer bags or airtight containers. Label the bags or containers with the herb type and date of freezing for easy identification.
7. Utilize Herb Cubes: When you need to use herbs in your recipes, simply grab the desired number of herb cubes from the freezer. Add them directly to soups, stews, sauces, or any other dish that requires herbs. The frozen herb cubes will defrost quickly, releasing their flavors and enhancing your culinary creations.

Tips for Freezing Herbs in Ice Cube Trays:

- Blanching: Some herbs, such as basil, benefit from blanching before freezing. Blanching involves briefly immersing the herbs in boiling water, followed by an ice bath, to help retain their vibrant color and flavors.
- Pre-Portioned Bags: If you know the amount of herbs you typically use in a recipe, you can pre-portion them in freezer bags before freezing. This way, you can easily grab the desired quantity of herbs without defrosting more than you need.
- Herb Combinations: Consider freezing herb combinations in separate ice cube sections. This allows you to have ready-made herb blends, such as basil and oregano or rosemary and thyme, for specific recipes.

By freezing herbs in ice cube trays, you can preserve their flavors and aromas, ensuring a fresh supply of herbs all year round. This gardening hack helps you reduce waste, conveniently store herbs, and effortlessly incorporate them into your culinary creations whenever you desire.

#93 Regrow kitchen scraps: Some vegetables like celery and lettuce can be regrown from the base.

The Regrowing Kitchen Scraps Hack: Sustainable Gardening at Your Fingertips

Instead of throwing away kitchen scraps like celery bottoms or lettuce stumps, you can easily transform them into thriving plants through regrowth. This gardening hack allows you to reduce waste, enjoy a continuous supply of fresh produce, and embark on a rewarding gardening adventure. Here's how to regrow celery and lettuce from kitchen scraps:

Regrowing Celery:

1. Save the Celery Base: Cut off the base of a celery stalk, leaving about 2-3 inches of the bottom intact. Set aside the upper portion of the celery for culinary use.
2. Place in Water: Place the celery base, cut side down, in a shallow dish or glass jar with a few inches of water. Ensure the water covers the base without submerging the upper part.
3. Provide Adequate Light: Place the dish or jar in a well-lit area, preferably near a window with indirect sunlight. Celery requires sunlight to regenerate and grow.
4. Change Water Regularly: Change the water every few days to prevent bacterial growth and maintain freshness. Keep the base hydrated at all times.
5. Observe Growth: After a few days, you should notice new growth emerging from the center of the celery base. Roots will begin to form, and small leaves will appear. Over time, the new celery shoots will develop into a full plant.
6. Plant in Soil: Once the celery has developed a sufficient root system and new growth, transplant it into a pot or garden bed with well-draining soil. Ensure the plant receives ample sunlight and water it regularly.

Regrowing Lettuce:

1. Save the Lettuce Stump: Cut off the bottom of a lettuce head, leaving about 1-2 inches of the stump intact. Make sure to retain the larger outer leaves for consumption.
2. Place in Water: Fill a shallow dish or jar with a small amount of water. Submerge the lettuce stump in the water, ensuring the cut side is facing down. The water level should cover the base without completely submerging the

upper part.

3. Provide Adequate Light: Place the dish or jar in a well-lit area with indirect sunlight. Lettuce thrives in cooler temperatures, so avoid exposing it to direct sunlight or heat sources.
4. Change Water Regularly: Change the water every few days to maintain freshness and prevent bacterial growth. Keep the stump hydrated throughout the regrowth process.
5. Observe Growth: After a few days, you should notice new leaves sprouting from the center of the lettuce stump. As the leaves grow, you can harvest them for consumption while allowing the plant to continue regrowing.
6. Transplant or Harvest: Depending on your preference, you can either transplant the regrown lettuce stump into a pot or garden bed with well-draining soil, or you can continue harvesting individual leaves for consumption as they mature.

Tips for Regrowing Kitchen Scraps:

- Patience is key: Regrowing kitchen scraps takes time, so be patient and observe the gradual growth of your new plants.
- Maintain consistent moisture: Keep the water levels in the dishes or jars consistent to ensure proper hydration for the regrowing scraps.
- Transplant to soil: Once the regrown plants have developed roots and sufficient growth, transplant them into soil for optimal growth and productivity.
- Enjoy fresh produce: Continually harvest and enjoy the regrown celery or lettuce leaves as they mature, ensuring a continuous supply of fresh greens.

By regrowing kitchen scraps like celery and lettuce, you embrace sustainability, reduce waste, and cultivate a closer connection to the food you consume. This gardening hack allows you to witness the regenerative power of plants and enjoy the satisfaction of nurturing them from kitchen remnants to thriving produce.

#94 Always keep learning: Gardening is a lifelong journey of learning, enjoy every step!

The Lifelong Learner's Gardening Hack: Cultivating Knowledge for Green Success

In the world of gardening, there is always something new to discover, techniques to master, and wisdom to gain. Embracing the mindset of a lifelong learner in gardening not only enhances your skills and knowledge but also opens doors to endless possibilities. Here's why continuous learning is vital in gardening and how to make it a part of your green journey:

1. Expand Your Gardening Repertoire: By continuously learning, you broaden your gardening repertoire. Explore new plant varieties, experiment with different techniques, and venture into unfamiliar gardening realms. This expands your horizons, enriches your gardening experiences, and adds diversity to your garden.
2. Stay Updated on Latest Practices: Gardening practices and techniques evolve over time. By staying updated through learning, you can adopt the latest innovations, sustainable methods, and efficient approaches. This empowers you to garden more effectively, achieve better results, and adapt to changing environmental conditions.
3. Problem-Solving and Troubleshooting: Learning equips

you with problem-solving skills to tackle gardening challenges. Whether it's combating pests, diagnosing plant diseases, or addressing soil issues, continuous learning provides you with the knowledge and resources to identify problems and find effective solutions.
4. Maximize Efficiency and Productivity: Learning helps you optimize your gardening efforts and maximize efficiency. Discover time-saving techniques, smart watering strategies, and efficient planting methods. This allows you to work smarter, not harder, and reap greater rewards from your gardening endeavors.
5. Environmental Stewardship: As a lifelong learner in gardening, you become an advocate for environmental stewardship. Stay informed about sustainable gardening practices, water conservation methods, and wildlife-friendly approaches. By implementing eco-friendly techniques, you contribute to the preservation and health of our planet.
6. Connect with the Gardening Community: Learning connects you with a vast community of passionate gardeners. Engage with fellow enthusiasts through local gardening clubs, online forums, or social media platforms. Share your experiences, exchange ideas, and learn from the collective wisdom of other gardeners.
7. Cultivate Curiosity and Joy: Gardening is a never-ending journey of discovery and joy. Embrace the spirit of curiosity and wonder by continually learning about plants, ecosystems, and gardening lore. Uncover the fascinating intricacies of nature and nurture a lifelong love affair with the beauty and science of gardening.
8. Embrace Learning Resources: Tap into an array of learn-

ing resources, such as books, online articles, podcasts, workshops, and gardening courses. Visit botanical gardens, attend gardening events, and participate in seed swaps to further enrich your gardening knowledge.
9. Reflect and Evaluate: Regularly reflect on your gardening experiences and evaluate the outcomes. Assess what worked well and what could be improved. Incorporate feedback and lessons learned into your future gardening endeavors for continuous growth and refinement.
10. Pass on Knowledge: As you continue to learn, share your knowledge with others. Mentor novice gardeners, engage in community outreach programs, or start a gardening blog. By passing on your expertise, you contribute to the growth and development of the gardening community.

By embracing the mindset of a lifelong learner in gardening, you embark on an enriching journey of self-discovery, growth, and green success. Embrace continuous learning, and watch your garden flourish while your own skills and knowledge blossom alongside it.

15

Conclusion

As we bid farewell to the captivating world of "94 Gardening Hacks," we do so with hearts brimming with inspiration and hands eager to get back to the soil. We have traveled through the seasons, unveiling the secrets of soil enrichment, unlocking the art of garden design, conquering the challenges of pests and diseases, and embracing the communal spirit of gardening. Our journey has been one of discovery, empowerment, and transformation—a testament to the enduring allure of nature's embrace.

But our exploration does not end here. It is merely a stepping stone, a prelude to a lifelong love affair with the earth and its bountiful offerings. Armed with the 94 gardening hacks we have encountered along the way, you are now equipped with an arsenal of knowledge, wisdom, and innovation. With each seed you sow, each blossom you nurture, and each harvest you reap, you will continue to deepen your connection to the natural world and cultivate a sanctuary of beauty and abundance.

Gardening is a dance—an intricate choreography of sunlight, water, and earth. It is a testament to our innate connection to the cycle of life, reminding us of our role as stewards of the land. Through our endeavors, we not only cultivate gardens but cultivate ourselves, nurturing patience, resilience, and a profound appreciation for the miracles that unfold beneath our fingertips.

As you embark on your gardening adventures, remember that the journey is as important as the destination. Embrace the joy of discovery, relish in the small victories, and learn from the inevitable setbacks. Nature is a patient and generous teacher, revealing her secrets in due time and rewarding our efforts with beauty, sustenance, and a sense of belonging.

But beyond the personal gratification, let us remember that gardening is a gift we can share. It is a language that transcends boundaries, cultures, and generations. As you embark on this journey, reach out to fellow gardeners, share your knowledge, and celebrate the collective wisdom that has been handed down through the ages. Create spaces of communal growth, where friendships bloom alongside vibrant flowers, and where the bonds forged in the soil nourish both the body and the soul.

In the pages of "94 Gardening Hacks," you have glimpsed the extraordinary potential that lies within your grasp—a tapestry of colors, scents, and flavors that knows no bounds. So, with renewed passion and purpose, step outside, dig your hands into the earth, and let your garden become a canvas for your dreams.

May your garden be a sanctuary of serenity, where the gentle rustling of leaves and the vibrant hues of flowers invite tranquility and inspiration. May it be a refuge for all creatures, great and small, where the delicate balance of nature is preserved and cherished. And may it be a testament to the resilience of life, a testament to our capacity to nurture and create, even in the face of adversity.

As you bid adieu to "94 Gardening Hacks," carry with you the spirit of curiosity, the joy of discovery, and the profound respect for the intricate dance of life unfolding in your garden. Embrace the ever-unfolding wonders of nature, for they are the wellspring of inspiration, solace, and rejuvenation.

Now, go forth, dear gardener, and may your journey be forever intertwined with the magic and beauty of the natural world. Embrace the transformative power of gardening, and let your hands sow the seeds of a brighter, greener future. For in the garden, dreams take root and miracles blossom, revealing the profound truth that we are not mere observers of nature but active participants in its eternal symphony.

About the Author

Welcome to 94 Gardening Hacks! My name is Travis Wilder and I'm so excited to be writing and sharing this book with you. It's a compilation of 94 gardening tips and tricks that can take your garden and gardening skills to a whole new level. Whether you're totally new to gardening and trying it for the first time or you're a seasoned gardener looking to add to your storehouse of knowledge, this book is sure to enhance your gardening skills.

The other reason I'm so bonkers about this subject is that I have a deep passion for all facets of gardening and growing stuff. I love to experiment when it comes to gardening. Sometimes I succeed; sometimes I fail. No big deal. It's all part of learning.

A brief background about me. Ever since I was a clumsy kid growing up in southeast Wisconsin, I loved growing things. In fact, I always had a deep interest in life and living things. I was a bit of a science geek in school, so I loved biology and the life sciences. I majored in biology in college. When you have a passion for something, you throw yourself at it lock, stock, and barrel. So, studying science was a labor of love.

I also attended Oregon State University where I studied Permaculture Design. But, that's a topic for another book.

I've since had the great fortune to try my hand at planning and growing gardens, orchards, edible landscapes, to the amazement and disbelief of some of our neighbors and family members. We have over 500 trees and shrubs on our property. Everything from the usual apples and pears to pecans, English walnuts, paw-paws, persimmons, and almonds. Oh yes, and gardens on top of gardens. I refer to myself as a psycho-farmer. Did I mention I love to grow things?

So, I've been a life-long resident of the great state of Wisconsin. I live here with my awesome wife and a cat we inherited from the kids. We live in a rural area with cows and chickens for neighbors. It's very peaceful here. It's given me the opportunity to try my hand at growing many different plants, trees, vines, you name it. And this book is an opportunity for me to share with you what I've learned and experienced first hand. Let's get growing!

Printed in Great Britain
by Amazon